I SHOULD BE DEAD...

Instead They Call Me
the Godfather

I SHOULD BE DEAD...

Instead They Call Me
the Godfather

SÖREN SÖRBO SAMUELSSON

Published by Best Seller Publishing®, St. Augustine, FL
Best Seller Publishing® is a registered trademark.
Printed in the United States of America.

ISBN: 978-1-966395-00-3

This publication is designed to provide accurate and authoritative information with regard to the subject matter covered. It is sold with the understanding that the publisher is not engaged in rendering legal, accounting, or other professional advice. If legal advice or other expert assistance is required, the services of a competent professional should be sought. The opinions expressed by the author in this book are not endorsed by Best Seller Publishing® and are the sole responsibility of the author rendering the opinion.

For more information, please write:
Best Seller Publishing®
1775 US-1 #1070
St. Augustine, FL 32084
or call 1 (626) 765-9750
Visit us online at: www.BestSellerPublishing.org

Table of Contents

Dedication

It is with a mourning heart that I dedicate this book to my lovely wife, Winnie, who went to be with the Lord on December 20, 2023, and to my dear twin brother, Leif Samuelsson, who also went to be with the Lord on January 24, 2024. Though they did not see this book published, they still live on in its pages.

I love you both, and you will be greatly missed by our families but we shall see one another again.

Introduction

Maybe we all have had the same thought: that I should have made a different decision. Or been struck in circumstances that should have cost us our lives, and yet we are still here to talk about it. Or maybe it's just a few of us — all I know is that I made some decisions and engaged in actions that brought me very close to my death. Even now, the health I enjoy is nothing short of a miracle — but wait, I am getting ahead of myself. Let me back up and start from the beginning.

My name is Sören Sörbo Samuelsson. I was born in Sweden on April 25, 1947. Okay, that may be too far back, but it is a good starting point. I had one twin brother, Leif Erick Samuelsson. My parents are Erick Slars and Anna-Greta Samuelsson. These are the facts, but in this book, I'm going to tell you my stories, stories that will show you where I came from and what has brought me to where I am now. There is more than one story that should have ended with my headstone; some of them are funny, some are sad. Some of them don't make me look good, but some of them make me look like a genius. That would probably be because of my dozens and dozens of inventions that are leaders in the window cleaning industry. All of those stories are part of who I am — the Godfather in our industry and a servant in life.

I hope you enjoy my book. At the end, I give you some groundwork for launching your own business. It is truly my goal to have everyone use the knowledge and wisdom that I was able to gain on this road that we all travel together.

I was born right after World War II. My dad was drafted into the army to protect the border around Sweden. Sweden was a neutral country and never suffered casualties. The war ended in September 1945. Nineteen months later, my twin brother, Leif, and I were born in a small industrial town named Borlänge, 186 miles north of Stockholm.

My mom and dad actually got together in 1943 when my dad was discharged from the military. They met at the local café in Ornäs, close to where my grandma and grandpa lived with my mom and her sister.

An old drawing depicting the search for King Gustav Vasa, on display in the Ornässtugan museum. Ornäs is a very interesting place. This is where the Danish soldiers were looking for Vasa when he was gathering an army of people to establish Swedish sovereignty, independent of Denmark.

When my brother and I were born, my mom was very sick and almost passed away. The doctor didn't think she would survive the delivery and did a cesarean section. We were never told who came out first. Mom didn't want us to fight about it growing up. The doctor had my grandma, grandpa, and dad by my mother's side, just in case she passed away, but she had healthy twin babies, and she survived the delivery.

Part I

My Younger Years

1950: Early Recollections

My twin brother, Leif (left), and me (right) as babies.

Leif (left) and me (right) with our bicycles.

My father in uniform.

My parents when they were dating (1943).

The first memory I have of growing up was when Mom put us to bed. I remember it was bright and sunny outside in the summertime because we had the midnight sun. She used to read a prayer with us. It seems kind of surprising to me when I think about it in my later years because no one in our family ever went to church. Later on, when I was starting to walk, I remember that I used to look out the window, and after that, Mom put us to bed. Though it was evening, it looked like it was the middle of the day, so I couldn't sleep. I had a little habit. I started biting the leaves on the potted plants in the window. My mom had a green thumb, and in Sweden, you have a shelf inside every window. She would have eight beautiful plants growing. This particular window had a flower with some really big, delicious green leaves. For some reason, I liked to chew them, and you could see the imprint of my teeth. I still don't know why I had an appetite for them.

During the wintertime, it was dark all day. I remember having to go to the outhouse sometimes late in the evening when there was 3 feet of snow, and it was freezing cold. I hated that! We did not have any bathrooms in the house, and when Mom was bathing us, we had to sit in a rectangular galvanized steel bucket that was heated up by being placed on top of the wooden stove in the kitchen. I still remember how cold it was!

I also remember looking at children's books that my mom purchased, and in one of those stories, there was a Black little boy. I was so excited about this boy. It was the first time I had seen a Black kid, and I told my mom I wanted to be like this boy. I wanted to be Black, and I was weeping because I had such a strong feeling that I wanted to be like him. Well, the closest I got was the nickname "Mexico," so I suppose I had to be satisfied with that later on in my life.

1952: Stealing Something Shaped My Life

When I was six years old, my brother and I started kinder-garten. I learned how to tie my shoelaces before my brother did, and I always had to help him with his shoes. I also remember I enjoyed kindergarten because we were learning how to paint with water-based paint. Every day, the teacher would mix water-based paint powder. She used a tiny little spoon to pour it into a glass of water and mix it. I thought that spoon was so cute that one day, my sticky fingers took that spoon home. I started to play with that little spoon at home, and it didn't take long before my mom realized I had something that she hadn't bought. She knew it came from the kindergarten school. Consequently, this is where I first learned how it feels when you want to die. My mother told me that I could not take anything that didn't belong to me. She told me to take it back, give it to the teacher, and ask her for forgiveness (a good lesson to learn). This incident shaped my life, and I never stole again. I still remember today how painful and difficult it was to go to the kindergarten the next day. The real reason I did it was because I was scared to death to go back home without obeying my mom's order. I knew exactly what my mom would say to me — "I am going to tell Dad when he comes home from work" — and that would have been a far worse situation. I still remember that lesson to this day, even though I'm approaching 80 years old! That lesson is still in my subconscious.

At an early age, I started to have ear infections once a year. It was always in wintertime, and it was very painful. I remember holding my mom's hand, and she would tell me to squeeze it really hard, which seemed to comfort me a little bit. At the right moment, when the eardrum was fully ripe and ready to explode, the doctor told me it was time to come into the hospital, and he would poke a hole in my eardrum and empty the pus. After a few years, the eardrum got so thin that it actually burst by itself. This condition followed me all the way up to second grade in school. At this time, I had my tonsils removed. I still remember I was so happy because the doctor prescribed ice cream following the operation.

1953: Ominous Indicators

My mom was the one who raised my brother and me. She had a special way of looking at us that was very powerful. It felt like she was looking right through us, so we obeyed immediately. I remember one time Mom had been vacuuming the floor, and she left the room. I figured out how to start the vacuum cleaner, and I spotted a bucket full of water. I thought it would be exciting to suck it up with the vacuum cleaner. As soon as I started to lower the hose into the bucket of water, my mom came back in and caught it in time. Today, I'm grateful for that.

Leif (right) and me (left) in our highly desired buffalo-skin jackets.

In those days, all the moms were homemakers, and the dads were the breadwinners. As a result, my mom always kept an eye on my brother and me. We had a wood-burning stove where we cooked everything. Every morning, my parents had to start a new fire using a box of matches they kept on the shelf. One day, I went out into the shed and made a little fireplace, put some sticks in there, and started a fire. My mom obviously saw the smoke coming out of the door and ran out of the house to stop me. She took me into the house, and I vividly remember sitting on her lap, getting scolded. I felt so bad about what I had done, I actually started to hit myself in the head. I felt like I wanted to punish myself. I found out later that I was a little bit suicidal, and sometimes it comes back to haunt me. It's a terrifying feeling!

1954: Very Strict Upbringing

The railroad station from my childhood. Picture taken in 2013.

Both my parents were good people. They didn't drink alcohol, they didn't smoke, and they didn't swear. My dad was a hardworking, very talented man. He could make anything, it seemed like. As an artist, he painted a lot. Additionally, he worked for the railroad, where he ended up working his whole life. As I said earlier, my mom was a homemaker. She was an excellent cook and was always baking pastries for when we had company over for coffee. My dad was a very quiet man. Every time my brother and I did something that we shouldn't do, Mom always reminded us that she would tell Dad when he came home from work. To us, he was a very scary person! Physical love was not shown in our house. Looking back, we were raised very strict. I never remember receiving a hug or any encouraging words. I suppose that's the way you grew up when you came from the Viking countries. I had a feeling that I was never good enough. I'm sure they meant well, but it backfired with me. I grew up with very low self-esteem.

1954: Feeling Like Singing

During the '50s, rock 'n' roll grew in popularity, and I felt like I wanted to sing. The songs I heard were from a pirate station broadcasting out in the ocean near Luxembourg. They were English songs, and they sounded so much better than Swedish songs. Every night, my brother and I would listen to this station before we went to sleep, and my mom would turn the radio off once we were asleep. I remember I felt like singing, and one evening, I shut myself in the bedroom. I started singing my heart out even though I didn't know English. I was singing similar words, but it was like speaking in tongues, I suppose. To my disappointment, my dad came running in, screaming at me to stop screaming! He said it sounded terrible! That was the end of my singing career. It took around 40 years before I started to sing again! I will tell you more about that later in the book (but if you have children who like to try something new, please support them).

1955: Starting First Grade in School

My first-grade class on the playground with our school behind us.

When my brother and I turned eight years old, we were enrolled in first grade. I realized very quickly that I didn't really care for school that much. One thing I realized I liked: girls. One day, I was running after a girl, and she slammed the door in front of me. The window broke, fell out, and landed on my nose bone, with blood splashing everywhere. The teacher had to rush me to hospital, and they had to sew a few stitches. I can still see the bump on my nose where the glass cut it. I don't have the nose structure my dad has anymore. His nose is like a ski jump, and because of this fracture, my nose is a little bit straighter. Actually, it turned out really good!

As I mentioned earlier, I never got any attention at home. Consequently, I did some crazy things so the girls would notice me. During the recess break, I jumped out the window on the third floor, where there was a gutter around 15 inches wide. The kids used to throw tennis balls and they were lying there waiting for me to rescue them. All the girls down below started weeping because they thought I would fall and die. However, I cleaned up the gutter and threw all the tennis balls down. I felt like a hero for the day. I got into trouble and I had to stand in the corner for ten minutes next break, but I felt good. I achieved something I hadn't before.

My dad worked at the railroad all his life, and because of that, my family was able to ride the train for free. Some of our most joyful times were when Mom, my brother, and I took the train to see our grandma and grandpa in Ornes. They were very nice people. Every time we visited their house, the birds landed on my shoulder. My grandpa was always feeding them, so they were tame. There was also a brown squirrel that would come down from the trees to get food.

My grandparents lived in a very small upstairs two-bedroom apartment. I remember there was a small kitchen where my brother and I slept in a rollout bed. It was very scratchy because there was hay in the mattress. In the morning, it would be flattened. The railroad tracks were only 300 feet from the house, and we could hear the train going by every morning. I liked to listen to the train.

My aunt lived in one of the small bedrooms. She was dating the man who would later become our uncle. He was from Poland, and during the war, he was captured by the Russians and arrested, and then shipped off to a concentration camp in Siberia. Thankfully, my uncle and two other men escaped and came to Sweden, where he met my aunt. I will never forget Uncle Walter because he had the first car in our family. It was a Jowett Javelin. They were manufactured by Jowett Cars, Ltd. in Great Britain and Australia from 1947 until 1953.

My aunt in the Jowett Javelin.

In 1953, Uncle Walter left for New York, where he started to work in a machine shop to save up money to bring my aunt to America. Two years later, in 1955, my aunt was ready to leave. I still remember when she left. In those days, immigrants traveled back and forth on ocean liners. We didn't see her again until we were 16 years old when she came home to visit. They lived in Brooklyn, New York, and later on moved upstate to the Catskill Mountains, where they purchased the Hudson Valley 9W Motel near the Hudson River. They never had any children, so my aunt used to send presents from America to my brother and me. I will never forget when she sent a couple of buffalo-skin biker jackets with a lot of chrome stars. We were the most popular kids in school! I have never seen a jacket like that, except in the movies. There were actually kids at school who wanted to buy those jackets from us. We wore them for many, many years. We were always excited to receive presents from our aunt, and we were always so proud to have somebody in America.

1956: Two Years in the Same Class

When the teacher started to give us homework, I realized I had a memory problem. My parents were very strict, and we always had to do our homework before we could go out and play. We had to memorize more and more things, and my mom would always go over the homework with us to see if we could remember what we had learned. I started to feel mentally stressed, especially trying to learn the mathematics times tables. I still don't know them! We had to learn them by memory.

I still remember I had to sit on the chair in the kitchen for hours and keep reading. My mom would then ask me the questions, but I'd already forgotten the answers. Well, I can't say I'd forgotten because I'd never learned them to begin with! This was very stressful for me, and I felt really bad about it. I learned to dream away, pretending I was reading even though I could hear my dad ridiculing me. As a result, I very seldom got to play, and I also started to feel anger toward him.

I feared going to school so much that I developed a sleep disorder from the stress. I had tremendous nightmares, and I also started to walk in my sleep. I remember waking up in the middle of the kitchen floor, sweating and scared to death! My mom used to ask me what I had been dreaming about, and I still remember the dream today. I could see myself in a big chunk of gel, and I could not escape! It was a very scary experience. Every day, walking to school, I feared that the teacher would ask me some question about the homework that I couldn't remember. It was a heartbreaking time. This feeling would never go away and has followed me throughout my life. I wish my mom had homeschooled us instead. Many people do that today because they think some of the things kids are taught in public school are terrible.

1957: Painting: The Escape from Reality

Creating art as a young boy.

A pencil illustration of a nightmare that I drew as a child.

I started to paint when I was very young. I got that talent from my dad because he was a well-known artist in our part of the country. He was always painting. I can still remember that oil paint smell, which I loved. Interestingly enough, in my paintings, people could see my frustration crying out. I was painting horrible-looking creatures in black and very dark colors. I would paint creatures in the shape of spiders with human heads. I remember my dad's art friends thought it was really good artwork. Painting became more and more my escape from the school nightmare.

I often find myself wondering about the actual cause behind my problems with memory. When I was only four years old, a neighbor girl pushed me in the swing that was hanging from the beam of our garage door opening. Unfortunately for me, she pushed me so hard that I tilted upside down and landed right on top of a nail sticking up in the entranceway to the garage. The nail went straight into the top of my head and into my brain. I like to blame my memory problem on that incident, LOL!!

It was so bad that one year, the teacher suggested to my mom that I would have to be retained and do the same school year one more time. However, my mom told the teacher that I would have to decide. My mom was nice enough to ask me if I would like to do that, and I said no! I was trying to get out of school, not add years to it! I was so embarrassed that I became a loner. I was always afraid that people would ask me something I couldn't answer. My painting was a way of escaping reality. Every time I painted, I entered a different world. Everything around me was gone. I didn't even hear when Mom told me that supper was ready.

1959: 13 Years Old

Another one of my childhood renditions of a nightmare.

My brother and I ended up being some of the taller kids in our school. Consequently, I was fairly good at playing hockey, which I loved very much! It was a rough sport and I liked that. I remember I had an accident playing hockey. This guy on the opposing team made a tremendous shot, and the puck landed right on top of my head. It was a professional-sized hard puck and I passed out. Unfortunately, it didn't give me my memory back. Maybe I got a little bit more crazy. I'm not sure. We had a hockey rink within walking distance of our house, so we played hockey just about every night during winter. In football, I always played defense because I loved the feeling of tackling someone! I participated in long-distance skiing and tried ski jumping, which was a disaster. I was trying to show my parents how brave I was by climbing up to the ski tower, but I didn't have those heavy-duty ski-jumping skis. I only had long-distance skis. I had practiced a few times, and then I invited my parents to come and watch me. I climbed to the top of the tower, and I took off down the jump, tucked down as low as possible to reduce wind resistance. When I finally reached the takeoff point, I flew straight out into the air, and the skis went up into the air in front of me. It was like hitting a brick wall. I don't remember how I landed, but I was rolling like a snowball down the landing strip! My parents said the snow was flying all around me. They couldn't even see me in this cloud of snow! Incredibly, I went up again three times with the same result. Ughhh! At least I tried and found out that ski jumping wasn't my cup of tea. Of course, my parents didn't think I was very good at it, but they thought I was brave to get up there, so high up. I suppose I'd done something good, but I never did it again.

My father and I before I attempted to prove myself with a ski jump.

I believe I would have been better off not going to school. I had bad grades throughout my school years, with the exception being an A in drawing. One time, I spent many days inside painting. I wasn't even interested in playing with my friends. As a result, my mom was worried about me. She was so concerned, she made me go out to play. However, painting was my way of escaping reality. When I was ten years old, people began to recognize my artwork, and I started to sell a few paintings to relatives and friends. I was thinking I would continue as an artist.

I also liked fishing. I would take my bicycle after school and paddle 8 miles out to Vassbo, where there was a little creek where I could fish for bass. I enjoyed that immensely (further on in the book, you will read about a miracle that occurred at this creek many years later).

Me in my teenage years.

A newspaper clipping with my artwork featured at the top, as well as a picture of me at my first job (second person from the right).

1962: 15 Years Old (Me and My Moped)

My first moped.

When I was 15 years old, I reached the age to legally ride a moped. I worked and saved some money and was able to purchase a used Puch (a German moped). I did a lot of extra chores so I could save up money to buy it. I always kept it clean and nice. I enhanced it by taking off the carburetor and modifying the piston by filing a half-moon in the bottom of the piston skirt so it would go faster.

I remember drawing motorcycles many times as a kid. It was at this time that the local newspaper discovered my painting talents and wrote an article about me as an up-and-coming young artist. All of a sudden, a man from the art academy came over to our house, offering me entrance into the art school. I had been thinking school was the worst place I knew.

I didn't want anything to do with anything remotely associated with school. During this time, I was more interested in motor-driven things. I wanted to build a go-kart and race. I gathered a bunch of steel tubing and started to hand-cut the tubing for the whole cart. Unfortunately, I never had enough money to weld them together, and to this day, I don't know what happened to the parts I made. What I remember is how much fun I had building something. The whole time I was building, I could see it finished in my mind, with a really cool-looking motor.

I was apparently pretty good with my hands. My family was not extremely poor, but we didn't have enough money to spare. Consequently, I always had to make my own toys, growing up. I became very handy because of that. When you're young, and you don't receive many things like other kids do, you become very upset with your parents. Now I realize that I learned a lot, and this is probably why, many years later, I have more patents in the window cleaning industry than all the other window cleaning manufacturers combined! It was this upbringing that encouraged me to invent so many new products through the years. I came up with these new ideas because I was a professional window cleaner, making prototypes for marketing projections — even making machines and jigs to produce these new products. I thank my mom and dad for this perseverance and for not spoiling me!

1963: 16 Years Old

The next year, my brother and I turned 16. We saved up money together to purchase a 1936 Harley-Davidson from Mats Hedberg, a very close school friend whom I had met in second grade at Domnarvets school. We sat side by side at the very back of the class because we were so noisy! We did that every grade up to the seventh grade, and some kids thought we were brothers. Many years later, I invited him to come to the U.S. He came over here one year after me, and we remained lifelong friends. Interestingly enough, we had a mutual interest in old cars, and we both worked on old cars all our lives.

Sadly, a few years ago, Mats passed away. I sure miss him. It was a tremendous loss for all of us, but 45 minutes before he passed away, I had the opportunity to lead him to Christ! Hallelujah!

My brother and I worked on the Harley-Davidson, but it needed a piston, and we didn't have enough money to fix it. Thankfully, I learned a lot from working on that bike, and later on, I paid my brother and kept the bike for many years, until I could afford to fix it.

1963: Getting into My First Fight

Outside of the town where I grew up was a place called Kvarnsveden. At this place, they always had live bands playing rock 'n' roll music in what was called the *Folkets Hus*, or Folk House. This was a place where young people gathered every Saturday. For a while, I had been watching some pot-smoking gangbangers downtown in Borlänge. One of these guys wore a big ring with a very big black stone in it that you couldn't miss. It could have been brass knuckles. On one particular Saturday night, I ran into these guys walking into the dance hall.

They obviously had noticed me because they approached me in a rather aggressive way. When I got closer to them, one guy bumped into me, and I got extremely upset. I noticed the big ring, and I told him with some not-so-friendly four-letter words to be careful he didn't sleep on his face with that big ring and hurt himself. In Sweden, it is common to see guys fighting like that because it was just the thing to do when you were young and hanging around downtown. Every time you got involved in an argument, they'd always say, "Let's settle this behind the building in the Duell." This guy said to me, "I'll see you behind the building in thirty minutes to beat you up."

This was the first time I'd been at this dance place, and I didn't know too many people. I knew one thing for sure: I had to face the music. Consequently, 30 minutes later, outside in the middle of the winter ice and snow with dancing shoes on, I prepared to get ready to fight. Additionally, during those 30 minutes, rumors had spread, and some people came to tell me they hoped I'd beat that idiot up! He was obviously not very well-liked. Soon enough, I had a guy coming to tell me, "He's waiting for you outside at the back." It wasn't even 30 minutes. Wherever did the time go?

I walked down the stairway and outside the building. At the back, I was surprised to see around 25 people out there standing in a ring, with him in the middle. We had an audience already. I'd had a couple of sips of cheap wine, so I felt pretty good. I didn't expect to have more than one guy trying to beat me up — but thankfully, they were just bearing witness. As I approached him, I wanted to throw the first punch right in his face! When I got to him, he lifted his arm, looked at his watch, and said, "You're late."

At that point, I loaded up and hit him right in the face. He flew backward, and I jumped right on top of him and kept on beating him up. Surprisingly, no one else got involved. Quicker than I'd expected, a couple of security guards came running and separated us, officially ending the fight. Many months later, I ran into him downtown, and he started fighting me again! That time, I beat him up really good, so he couldn't even walk. Before we were separated, he told me that he would get his whole gang and beat me up. It never happened. As a result of that, I got some new friends from the audience. I remember I was very proud of myself, and it felt good. This was just the beginning; there would be many more fights later on when I got around in my American car.

1963: Alcohol Came into My Life

When I was around 16 years old, I started to hang out with older guys. On one occasion, I went over to one of my buddies' houses. His parents were gone for the weekend, and my friend opened up his dad's bar, and we started drinking vodka. This was actually my first time drinking alcohol. I remember my buddy's neighbor was a lot older and already drinking. We were sitting at the kitchen table pouring the alcohol into two glasses on the table, and for some reason (I had had a few drinks already), I felt like hitting my hand on the table. To our surprise, after I hit the table, both of the half-filled glasses flew up into the air and landed upside down. The drinks were still in the glasses, slowly leaking out between the table and the rim of the glass. I remember we were looking at one another, like, *Is this real?* I can still see it in my mind; we were all very surprised.

I realize now that the alcohol made me aggressive, and that was the start of a different lifestyle. This aggressive behavior would get me into a lot of trouble later on in life. I finally felt no fear. Strangely, I had feared my parents all my life. When I finished seventh grade, my mom insisted that my brother and I do one more grade. My school years were a nightmare for me. Just my terrible luck, the school had started to offer a new grade: Eighth grade. My brother and I enrolled in this new eighth-grade class. I don't know why I did it. Probably because we grew up in fear of our parents and we obeyed anything our mom said. I didn't have strength enough to stand up to my parents. It's hard to explain how a person could get so much power over someone else.

1963: Getting into the Working Life

During my eighth-grade year, the school gave students the opportunity to try a different kind of work during the school year. Since the only thing that I excelled at was drawing pictures and painting, my mom and dad suggested that I take advantage of that, and I started to practice at Domus department store in Borlänge. It was at the department store where I got the opportunity to work on my artistic skills. My dad's artist friend — the one who had come over to our house to look at my paintings when I was younger — was the supervisor of the art department. I was painting those horrible monsters, and for this reason, I got that school practice job. I remember being in the storefront hanging up signs, and there were wires sticking out from the wall. I probably expected it to be 220-volts, but I still wanted to find out. My curiosity got the best of me. I grabbed those two wires, and it was a 220-volt tremendous handshake. I needed to know what 220-volts would feel like, I suppose? I worked in that department store for a couple of years, and in the mornings before I started, I also worked on a delivery truck, delivering fish to all the stores downtown. A very smelly business! After a couple of years, I didn't really feel like that was my future, so I quit.

1964: Working in a Steel Factory

The local steel factory was the third-biggest steel factory in Europe. It had around 2,000 employees. The first job I got was at the band-slitting machine, where my job was to wrap steel wire around sheet metal rolls. My working shifts started at 4 a.m. and went to 12 noon, and the next week, they were from 12 noon to 8 p.m. When I worked the morning shift, I realized that the prevailing work ethics were not really what I had expected.

Every morning, the shift boss and the workers would lie down to sleep for a couple of hours before the day shift showed up at 6:45 a.m. So, we went to sleep every morning, but I had a hard time sleeping. When I worked the afternoon shift, to my surprise, the workers played tennis and bowling right after the day shift foreman left at 4:30 p.m. I never would have dreamed that people would work this way in the factory! However, this was the only place that this occurred, I found out later.

After working there for two years, I developed arthritis in my wrists. As a result, the factory's doctor started rotating me among different departments. I learned a lot by constantly switching. I worked in the rolling mills department, turning over red-hot railroad tracks with a 6-foot-long steel fork. I remember one time when I started that task, the railroad track came out of the rolling mills red-hot, and I was supposed to turn it over with the fork. The track got stuck, and when they pulled it into the rolling mill again, it twisted, and the steel fork hit me right on my jaw. I'm surprised I didn't pass out, and I couldn't get a word out of my mouth for a few minutes!

Subsequently, I got tired of that position, so I went back to the doctor, who assigned me to another department. I got to know how to change departments; I wanted to try something else, so he sent me to the steel-melting department, where we produced steel. Sadly, I remember one night shift, one of my co-workers jumped into a 30-ton pot of molten floating steel, committing suicide.

Fortunately, I enjoyed this kind of rough work. If you have ever been in the steel-melting industry, you know it's dark all day long, but they have bright lights way up in the ceiling, up above where the traverses run back and forth. Everything is made of steel and red bricks. Because of the dark winters, I peddled my bicycle to work in the dark, worked in a dark building, and when I came out, I peddled home in the dark. Therefore, you lived in the dark for a few months, except on the weekends when you could experience the daylight.

In Sweden, everybody rides their bicycles to work because gas is so expensive. It's always 100 percent more than you'd pay in America! You would only drive your car on the weekend, during that time. After a few years, I was transferred to a different department, working at the railroad tracks where they would dock all the steel that was shipped to different places in the world. Swedish Sandvik steel was known for its high quality throughout the world. I would jump between carts in order to attach the big, heavy loop onto the big hook. It was extremely challenging as well as dangerous. If you weren't careful, you could be squashed in between those big bumpers that smashed together right behind your back. You had to be fast before the railroad carts would spring apart.

Also in 1964, I purchased a 1947 Chrysler Windsor coupe, the first car I purchased on my own. Because I was working, I was able to buy my own car, and it was gorgeous. It was excellent for cruising around town looking for girls. In earlier years, I had already purchased three different cars with my buddy Tommy Gardskog. The first one was a 1956 Mercedes-Benz, the second was a 1953 Volvo PV Sport, and the third one was a '57 Ford Fairlane coupe. We would go out drinking and partying every Saturday and Wednesday night. Wednesday was called Little Saturday. I was now drinking two days a week. I was a very shy person until I got a couple of drinks in me, and then my whole persona changed. I would sit in the passenger seat, drinking like we did in Sweden during the '60s, cruising around downtown Borlänge.

By now, I had been involved in a few street fights. Looking back on my childhood again, my parents had given my brother and me a very strict upbringing. I considered myself the black sheep of our family. This probably would have made literal sense because I had dark hair and my twin brother had blond hair. They called us *sotlug och linlug* in Swedish, which translates to "ash hair and white hair."

Through the years, I never felt any encouragement from my family. It seemed like everything was very negative, as I stated before. I had very low self-esteem. I didn't think very highly of myself. I was big for my age, and I hung out with older guys. They all had American cars from the '40s, '50s, and '60s. They took good care of them. All the way up until now, I have seen American cars in Sweden that I have never seen here in America. We would cruise around town, sometimes picking up girls, and then in a caravan, we would drive out to different places where they had Saturday night dances in the barns. I remember getting into another fight, and the next morning, when many of the guys had gathered down at the café talking about Saturday night's incident, one guy told me, "I didn't know you were that good a fighter." I'd never heard that before. It felt good. Because of my reputation, I got into more fights. I felt okay being known for something.

Once in Gagnef, there was this guy named Stafan Gote, who was known as a good street fighter. We fought, and he knocked me down real bad. He got a clean shot at my face, he knocked me to the ground, and he kept beating me until I passed out. I never got up from that one. I wanted revenge, and I kept looking for him downtown. The following weekend, I found him. As soon as we started fighting, the police showed up. For some reason, we never fought again. Many years later, we became friends when he came to visit me here in California. He even worked for me in my window cleaning company a few times throughout the years. But anyway, during those years in Sweden, I was working on my cars, and I learned a lot, even being able to take the engine out of the Chrysler and rebuild it.

1964: Going Downtown to a Maranatha Concert

During the '60s, there was a religious revival going on in Sweden, thanks to an evangelist named Målle Lindberg, who was touring around the whole country. Everywhere he went, there were big write-ups in the newspaper. This became a big joke because wherever he showed up, people bombarded him with raw eggs and tomatoes. One weekend, he came to my hometown, and one of my buddies said, "Let's get some eggs and tomatoes and join the party."

We ended up going to the Maranatha concert (a type of religious worship concert) at the folk park in downtown Börlange on Saturday, and a lot of people started bombarding Lindberg with eggs and tomatoes. Luckily enough, I was sober and driving the car that night, and I was not in the mood to throw any eggs. I will never forget when one egg hit him right on the forehead. That's when they led him off the stage, and the show was over. However, he got a lot of publicity because he knew what was going to happen before he came up on the stage. He became really well known all over the country due to the fact that he was on the front page of all the newspapers. He was a good singer, and many years later, after I became a born-again Christian, I had a chance to meet this famous evangelist. You will see later on in this book what happened at the radio station.

Part II
Big Changes in My Life

1965: My First Crush

Every Saturday, we went cruising in my '47 Chrysler in downtown Borlänge. One Saturday, I spotted a beautiful blond girl, Lilian, riding with a guy in a 1959 Dodge convertible. Many times, I'd seen her cruising around town with that guy. I noticed that she noticed me, too. I asked my buddy Bo Eriksson, who I'd known since I was 15 years old, "Have you seen that blondie in that convertible car?"

"Yeah, how can you not?" he said and laughed.

A month later, I believe on a Saturday, cruising around town in my Chrysler, I spotted the same blond girl and her friend, so I stopped and invited them for a ride around town. I had a big advantage living in Sweden in those days: I had a nickname that the girl knew. They called me "Mexico" because I had a darker complexion, as my dad's family was from France. And when you live in a country where everybody is blond, girls notice you. To make a long story short, that girl and I started dating.

We ended up having a seven-year relationship, and she gave birth to a beautiful baby girl.

(AUTHOR'S NOTE: For many years, I did not know her old boyfriend, but one time when, I came home to visit from America, I had the opportunity to meet him and his new wife. He's a very nice guy; his name is Per-Ake, and he has a sawmill in Dala-Floda, where he makes antique moldings from timber. Last week, I went over to buy all the moldings for the restoration of my house and we had a long, exciting talk about the things that had happened so many years ago. He remarried and has been married for 40 years. I also got remarried, and I've been married for 50 years to Winnie, and here we are meeting so many years later, talking about the past.)

It's very sad that my Lilian passed away a few years back. She was also a very nice person who didn't really have to leave us that early, but I still have our wonderful daughter, Anette, whom we had together, walking with her spirit. Winnie and Lilian were very close friends through the years. But anyway, back to the story.

Lilian lived outside town, in Dala-Floda, a 45-minute ride into the farmland. Every time I went to pick her up because I was an outsider, I was threatened by the local mob. My buddy Bose said to me, "We'd better put a steel pipe in our car before we go and get her, so we can defend ourselves." Well, we never had to use it.

I started to sleep over at her place. I actually drove my car without a driver's license for many years, as you will find out, and one morning, when I came out to start my Chrysler, the local guys had punctured a couple of my tires overnight. Soon I got my revenge! I beat up some of those guys. Years later, most of those guys became my friends. Soon my dream girl moved to my hometown, where we lived together.

I had an old friend of mine who had gone to the United States many years earlier with his parents. His name is Kenny. He came visiting that summer from California when we were going to Norway. He had already promised to drive my '47 Chrysler. I did not have a driver's license — I had to wait for two years before I could get one — so we took off to Oslo and camped above the town. It had a beautiful view of the city below.

One night, Kenny and my brother, Leif, took a ride downtown to Oslo and they came back on foot. The problem was, Kenny was only 16 years old, which was okay for driving in California but not in Norway. Luckily enough, my brother had just received his driver's license in the mail right after we left, so my mom sent it to Oslo, and we made it back home.

Lilian and I would joke often that we must have conceived our daughter during that trip, because nine months later, we had a beautiful baby girl. We were very happy together. To save money, I was building most of the furniture for our house in the wood shop that the company provided for its workers. I paid for the lumber, and I could use the machines to make furniture. At this time, I was still doing a lot of painting. Due to my handiness, I was able to build my own still, and so I was producing 96 percent alcohol in our kitchen every Saturday. This was the finest and strongest alcohol you could drink. It was explosive. I used to put a little drop of alcohol on top of the sink, light a match, and hold it 4 inches above the alcohol to see if it caught fire. I would stop cooking and make another batch.

1965: Drinking Buddies and Locomotives

At the factory, I'd changed departments a few times, and now I was stationed at the large railroad track. This was at the end of the smaller, narrow railroad track, which the company was going to close down in a year and replace with trucks instead. Every shift, we delivered all the melted lava left over from the steel-melting furnaces where I used to work a few years earlier. We transported it to the special dump where it would cool off. We had two teams. I was working in one of two locomotives, with an older man driving it. When we worked the night shifts, my two drinking buddies would be driving the second locomotive. Every night shift, they had a bottle of homemade booze. I used to go over to their locomotive engine and sit there and have a few drinks with them.

My chauffeur was very upset about this but too afraid to complain to me. However, one night when we went out to the dump, he tried to run me over with the train while I was hooking up in between the cars. Thankfully, he did not succeed, but I let him know what I was thinking about him. A year later, the railroad track was demolished, and they asked me if I would like to drive the new dump truck that would do the same job more easily. Of course, I said yes! This was a humongous V8 diesel truck, with a rumbling sound singing *made in America*. It was designed with two arms to lift a 30-ton pot of melted lava steel over the roof and put it in the back on a special bed designed for this big pot. It had fireproof bricks on the roof to prevent the molten lava from coming through the roof in case of a leak.

Anyway, I got the job even though I did not have a driver's license, which they did not know. I liked this job immensely. When I was 18 years old, I was in jail so many times that I had to wait for two years until I turned 20 before I could take a driving test. Finally, I got my driver's license, and then I lost it in six months! Here I was, driving the biggest truck in the whole factory, and nobody had ever asked if I had a driver's license! I loved it. One day, the foreman came to tell me a new guy was starting the next day, and he wanted me to train him. The next morning, the new guy showed up, and to my surprise, it was my old buddy who had tried to run me over with the train a year earlier!

Now, I was expected to teach him how to drive the truck. So, after he was introduced by the foreman, he climbed up the ladder and closed the door. I went to load up the first pot, lifting it up in the back of the truck. I got a bright idea! I remembered what he had done to me a year earlier. Thus, I decided it was my turn to get back at him. So after loading the truck, we started to drive down the road, and I knew exactly what to do. I stepped on the brakes while making a somewhat dangerous maneuver, and he started screaming, "Let me out of here!" It was the last time I saw him.

I grew tired of this job. I went back to the doctor, and he said that since I had been in this industry for seven years, he would send me to learn a new trade. I signed up for welding school. As a result, I had to move up north to a city called Mora. I was still doing artwork, and I did one pencil drawing that became my favorite — the only complete one I did during this time. I enrolled in a two-year machinist and welding course.

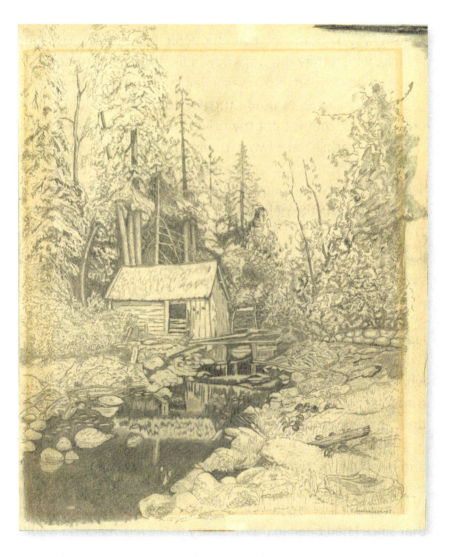

Pencil art from 1968.

NOV • 65 •

My friend (left) and I (right) sitting on my Chrysler coupe in 1965.

My Chrysler during a fishing trip. I'm petting the horse.

It was during this time that those popular Hell's Angels movies were showing in the movie theaters in Sweden. I got so excited about their lifestyle of riding a Harley-Davidson that I started to look around at the farms in my area for a World War II military Harley-Davidson. At one farm, I purchased a 1942 H-D that was all in parts. I needed extra money, so I started a lottery at the school. The problem was that the first prize was a bottle of vodka, and the teachers found out about it, and I was kicked out of the school. Thankfully, I had been there for a year and had already learned welding. So, I moved back home, and I had time to build my 1942 Harley-Davidson, which I finally got running. I painted it using spray cans; it looked pretty good.

When I was home, I did quite a bit of fishing. On one occasion, I was riding on a small island on my Harley-Davidson. I had 19-inch ape hangers on it and in the middle of my ride, the whole handlebar came off! Luckily, I was driving very slowly, so I didn't get hurt when I laid it down. One day, I took Lilian for a ride. The bike had a hard tail, and it didn't have any springs in the back seat. We were riding down the highway, and pretty soon, we hit a pothole. She flew up in the air and landed on the taillight. I think that was the only time she took a ride with me.

1968: A Near-Fatal Mistake

Art from the 1960s.

Another painting from the 1960s.

A painting from 1967.

In 1968, I signed up for a two-year car mechanic school in Hedemora. I was riding my 1942 Harley-Davidson back and forth every day, and it was around a two-and-a-half-hour ride each way. In those days, you didn't have to wear a helmet. Soon, I rented an apartment that I shared with one of my school-mates. The funny thing was that I was still driving without a driver's license! I also had a Volvo PV Sport that I took to school sometimes. One weekend, I decided to stay and party with my school buddy. Well, after a few drinks, feeling really good, I said, "Let's go to Avesta." And because we had been drinking, we decided to drive through the farmland on dirt roads.

After driving for a period of time, my buddy said, "I think the police are after us!"

"Well," I said, "let's shake them off," and I started to drive faster. All of a sudden, riding on a long, straight portion of road, we came upon a sharp curve. Our decision to drive on a dirt road was another mistake. As we were coming into the curve, I lost control of the car and crashed.

In lieu of a photograph, I drew this representation of my car accident.

When I woke up, I was lying on the side window in the back of the car, with the car lying on the driver side. I realized my body was not in the car, but the car was lying on the right side with the door open, holding the car up. The door was crumpled up, looking like a harmonica, and holding the car in a leaning position. This was definitely a near-death accident! I was able to crawl out through the door, underneath the car, and there was my drinking partner, lying there without any sign of life. I pulled him out from underneath the car and lay him on the side of the road in the grass. I looked around and saw a farmhouse up the hill. It was at this moment I realized that there was no police car following us. I ran up there, knocked on the door, and asked if they could call a taxi. I returned to my buddy to see if he was still alive, but he did not respond. He was still passed out. Unfortunately, instead of a taxi, I heard sirens coming in our direction. I sure did not want to blow in the balloon, so I lay down beside my friend! Fortunately, I passed out right away.

The next thing I knew, I heard voices, and it was the police. They said they wanted to ask me some questions. And I realized I was lying on the operating table at the hospital. Apparently, my head was wounded. I found out that a doctor was in the process of sewing it together. I could hear the nurses talking, and I heard the cops surrounding the operating table, waiting for me to come to. I kept my eyes closed, pretending that I was still passed out. I heard the nurse ask the doctor, "Should I numb him?"

The doctor said, "He won't feel anything," so they didn't use any anesthesia.

I woke up the next day, and the police were gone. What a miracle! I got released from the hospital at 6:30 in the morning and went down to the highway to hitchhike back home. All I had to wear was my bloody short-sleeved shirt and a pair of dirty Levi jeans. My shoes were still in the car, so I was barefoot. I was worried that nobody would want to pick me up, the way I looked. And I was two-and-a-half hours from home. But to my surprise, a delivery truck stopped and picked me up. The driver was a friend of a friend of mine. His name was Bosse. He was shocked to see me so far away from home, looking like I did. I told him the whole incredible story.

Interestingly enough, I went back a couple of days later and looked at the place where we had crashed the car. I looked at that post beside the road, and the marks on it were even higher than I'd thought. It was 5 feet up in the air, and of course, the car was totaled! It was totally squeezed together in the middle from the impact of the pole. The car looked like a peanut squeezed together in the middle. My name could have been written on a headstone. Of course, the police had had the car towed to a storage place, and it was there that I first saw the damage. I was home from school for a week.

Luckily, I had my 1942 Harley-Davidson, so I was driving that until I purchased another car. Soon thereafter, we moved up to Mockfjärd and lived there for a couple of years. There was a lot of friction between Lilian and me, and I realized that we were getting closer to separation because of my wild lifestyle.

My first motorcycle, a 1942 Harley-Davidson.

My friend Bo (left) and I (right) while I was putting the motorcycle together.

1969: Enlisting in the Army

As everyone was required to do, I had to enlist in army service in the city of Östersund, an eight-hour ride up north to Lapland, where the reindeer walk on the highways. I was not too excited about it. When I arrived, I ran into an old biker friend of mine from my hometown who had been there for seven months already. He was going home in two months. I told him I was going to get out before him. Soon after, I went to the doctor, and I complained about my old injury from the steel factory. I had all my doctor's papers, and they declassified me to the lowest military rank, where I joined my Buddy, Mats Heden. We started hanging out together. One night, we got into an argument, and he decided to stay downtown. He got into a fight and was arrested, blaming it on his mental health while at the police station. As a result, he ended up in a mental institution for a period of time. I also got into trouble getting into a fight at a bar. I had to pay my way out of that situation.

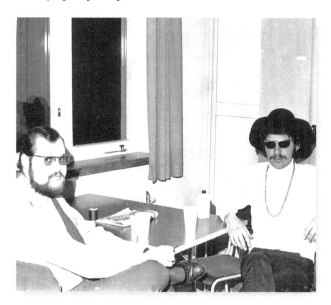

My army buddy Mats (left) and I (right).

On another night, after going on a date outside Sveg, one hour away from the base, on the way back to the base, I was driving too fast and hit some black ice, I believe. I crashed the car and ended up upside down in the middle of the forest on an ice-cold winter night. When I came to, I was freezing, so I tried to start the car when it dawned on me that the car was lying upside down on its roof, and I was lying on the ceiling. Because of the gasoline smell, I realized the car could catch fire. I assumed the gasoline was pouring out of the carburetor.

I was able to open the door and stick my leg outside the car, only to sink down into the snow. My pants slid up above my knees. As fun as this sounds, it was 20 below zero outside, and I had on my dancing shoes and a white nylon shirt. I was lucky it was a full moon, so I could see the road. I did not know which way to run, finally deciding to run in the direction from which I believed I had come. It was so cold outside that the breath from my mouth started to build ice on the side of my face! I was running as fast as I could, and all I could hear was the wind whistling in the forest. I was way out in the middle of nowhere, and I didn't see any homes or cars, just the howling wind to keep me company.

Another pencil illustration of that fateful night.

Finally, I spotted a house way up on the left side of the highway. My fingers, by this time, were so frozen I could barely move them. I knocked on the door, and a man opened it. I apologized for waking them up in the middle of the night. I could see his wife was very frightened in the background, peeking through the bedroom door. I explained that I needed a taxi and asked if I could use their phone. However, they would not let me come in. I had to stand outside, waiting for 40 minutes. I thought I was going to freeze to death. Good thing I had antifreeze in my blood. Finally, a taxi came. The driver had seen my car lying upside down and asked me if that was my car. I told him no; I'd been here having a good time with Mr. Anderson.

Of course, I just came up with that name (seven years later, something happened that I will explain later on in this book that will blow your mind). I lied, of course, and I'm sure he could hear from my dialect that I was from South Sweden. He said we should stop to look inside the car to make sure no one was injured inside. Unfortunately for me, he said that he had already called the police. Soon, we approached my car, 90 percent of which was lying upside down in the ditch, with the hood facing the forest and the trunk on the roadside. Well, he stopped and looked inside the car, only to find that it was empty. We continued to drive toward the army base, and all of a sudden, he said, "There are the police."

So the taxi driver slowed down and stopped. This stressed me out! I figured he was going to catch me now and arrest me for drunk driving. We stopped on the opposite side of the road, and the police officer came over and talked to the taxi driver. After speaking with the driver, he pointed his flashlight in my face in the back seat. I didn't say a word. The taxi driver told the police that I had come from a friend's house, and the officer allowed us to leave. I tell you, God was with me even though I didn't know Him! As soon as I got back to the army base, I jumped over the fence and went to bed immediately. Incredibly, I never heard from the police.

The next day, I had the car towed to the army base, still in running condition. I did everything I could to be disqualified from the army. Only two weeks before my friend was to go home, I managed to get my release (I had to produce some drastic event that I will not reveal at this time). My buddies couldn't believe that I'd managed to do what I'd told them I would do when I first enlisted. So, I packed up everything the next day and drove my car back home.

A pencil drawing of finally finding help after the accident.

1969: Driving off the Road Again

Amazingly, I was home for only a couple of weeks when I drove off the road again, but this time, I was flying in the air around ten feet off the ground, and landing on all four wheels beside the road in the snow. The next day, I called the tow truck.

The summer came, and Lilian and I separated. I went back to my hometown and started to work as a welder for Minko Maronof Welding Company. Minko was a hardworking Polish man from Barkagardet. As luck would have it, he had a little outside closet large enough for a single bed and nothing else. I lived there until I saved up enough money to rent an apartment. I had always been a hard worker, and I started to break records in welding production. My goal had always been to try to be fast. I remember thinking that I could weld without the welding helmet just to be faster and make more money. Regrettably, after only one week of doing that, I was blind due to burning my pupils. It feels like you have sand in your eyes. I went to the doctor, got some eye drops, and recovered after only two weeks!

I worked for Minko for two years, and then I met some other guys who worked for a big mechanic and welding company from Hallstahammar. They made very good money because they were traveling between different steel factories in Sweden. Thus, I applied, and I got hired. I made a lot more money. We were all very hard workers. There were no mechanics at the local factories who could keep up with us. We were very much liked by the companies for which we worked because they knew we got the job done a lot faster than their own mechanics. We were able to repair big industrial machines that weighed many thousand pounds. Also, we did a lot of welding construction where we were walking on I-beams, sometimes two stories high, without using safety lines. It was so much easier in those days because there weren't as many safety regulations.

The crew I worked with generated a lot of enemies at the places we worked since we did the jobs in a much shorter time frame than the local mechanics. It could be because many of them were so lazy. They didn't appreciate it when we exposed their laziness by showing their boss that the job could be done in half the time. I blended in well with this hard-living, hardworking bunch of guys. We were drinking almost every night. Even though we got paid every Friday, we were broke by Thursday. Unbelievably, one of the guys had to drink a pint of vodka every morning in order for his body to function. I noticed one Friday before he got paid, his face was swollen up, and his eyes were red and tearing because he hadn't had his pint of vodka that morning. He never appeared to be drunk. I could see for the first time in my life what alcohol did to a hardworking man. We didn't hold back at all. We were staying in extravagant hotels, more or less living like kings. Until we ran out of money.

One summer, my buddies and I tried something different. The company had rented summer cabins around a lake in the southern part of Sweden. It was actually a summer resort, but we stayed there one winter. There was a kitchen right beside the lake. We were there for a couple of months to repair some big industrial machines. The guys found out that I had built a still and made my own homemade alcohol. They asked me to bring it with me, and we decided to buy cleaning alcohol, called T-Sprit, from the gas station. Cleaning alcohol has a lot of alcohol in it. We decided to run it through my machine when we didn't have any money left for booze. I filled it, started it up, distilled out the alcohol, and it looked pretty good. And so we partied that night. The next day, people asked us what we had done. "You smell like T-Sprit!" our friends said. They could not even get near us because we stank so badly! We couldn't smell it, but it was the first and the last time we distilled T-Sprit from the gas station.

1969: Trouble with the Police

Once in a while, I visited my hometown. I came home to hang out with my brother, Leif, and our friend Kjell. One summer, we went to the Dala-Järna Flyg festival, where all the guys with their big American cars meet up every year. We liked going to it because we would get drunk and have a wild time. My brother, Leif, Kjell, and I decided to start drinking around noon. Around 5 p.m., somebody came and told me that the police had taken Kjell into custody for drunkenness. I immediately went up and confronted the five security guards who had apprehended him. I started to argue with them and told them that they had to let Kjell go because, I assured them, I would take care of him. All of a sudden, they jumped on me instead to arrest me as well. The officers tried to get me into the police van, but I resisted, and it escalated into a brawl. The officer was fighting with me to get me into that van. While this was happening, Kjell took the opportunity to run away. However, after a few minutes, they caught him and brought him back to the security van. When I saw that, I agreed to stop fighting and get into their van. I figured I could talk some sense into them. It was a 45-minute ride to the jail. There were five security guys in the van surrounding Kjell and me, with one on each side of us. Additionally, we were sitting in the middle, and we had one in front of us and two in the front seat. Interestingly enough, the one on the other side of Kjell was the one I was arguing with mostly, and he was making me more and more angry. He pushed the wrong button, and I took a long swing around Kjell and hit the officer right in the face. I found out later that I had broken his nose! Blood was splashing all over us, and immediately, the other three security guards threw themselves onto me. They sat on me all the way to the jail, where we spent the night. Well, a month later, I had to go to court. Thankfully, because it was my first offense, I got only a month in the correction facility in cold Majorshagen.

I was actually happy to do that because I could not get away from my drinking. It was probably not the ideal way to get sober from alcohol, but it worked. I was sober. While there, I learned from other inmates how to do tattooing, so I started inking my left arm. I got hold of three safety pins, tied them together at the end of a pencil, and I got some black ink. And there we go, just jabbing this needle in under the skin. Well, it wasn't 100 percent perfect, but once you do it, it's too late to change your mind.

It was pretty cool because, during the day, we were working in the forest as lumberjacks. It was, without a doubt, a lifesaving time for me. Unfortunately, I got out of prison and went right back to my wild lifestyle of women, booze, and partying! I still had my old job, so I continued to make a lot of money traveling all over Sweden. I worked in the silver and copper mines, repairing machinery. Of course, the mines had very good security control going in and going out; however, we got to know the local mechanics there, and we really wanted to have some pure silver and copper. We went down to the harbor and purchased American whiskey from the ships, and then we traded whiskey for silver and copper. This was in wintertime, and it was dark even in the middle of the day. But it was worth it: the money was good, and that's how I got enough money to go to California.

1970: California, Here We Come

A picture of me in my younger years.

My friends and me before I left Sweden.

Kenny, who five years earlier was driving my '47 Chrysler when we went to Oslo, Norway, eventually went back home to California. Well, he came back to visit us in Sweden after finishing his service in Germany. In 1970, he asked me, "Why don't you come to California and visit, now that you're single?" He told me, "It is summer all year round where I live."

"Wow, I would like that," I said. "I'll take you up on that."

I had really started to get tired of my lifestyle. The fighting started to get old, I was tired of paying so much in taxes, and it was time for a change. Thus, I told him that if I could find a warmer place than Sweden, I would move there in a heartbeat! I saved up enough money to take a nine-month vacation in Palm Springs.

1971: Leaving Cold Sweden, I Land in Palm Springs, California

I still remember walking up to a palm tree and touching the fronds, thinking it felt so amazing. Kenny had already told me that I could stay with him at his parents' house. I didn't want to stay there for free, so I started to pay rent right away. I think I learned that lesson growing up in my parents' house. When I started to work, my mom and dad said that I had to pay rent. So, both my brother and I paid rent when we started to work, but now I was living in this heavenly place, California. It had a summer heat I had never experienced before — 115–118 degrees during the day. Unfortunately, my money, which was supposed to last for nine months, was gone in six. We spent just about every night in the nightclubs, especially Jilly's and GiGi's nightclubs. It was a very exciting time in my life. You could see movie stars walking around like normal people in those days: Elvis Presley was seen walking with his bodyguards; Steve

McQueen was around town; you could see Bob Hope driving in his Rolls Royce; Frank Sinatra sometimes visited Jilly's; and very often, you saw *mafiosi* gathering at these nightclubs.

Well, my extreme lifestyle dried up my savings, and in order to stay, I had to look for a job. I landed a job at a welding shop but soon had to quit because I didn't speak English. I knew a man who had a window cleaning company, and he offered me a job as a window cleaner. I said to him, "I am a welder and a mechanic. How can I be a window cleaner? That is a job for women! Can you imagine me standing there with a little rag, wiping the windows off? No, I'm gonna look for a real man's job."

Thankfully, after failing to find a job but needing to make money, I was thinking *Well, maybe I can wipe those windows until I learn how to speak English.* So, with my tail between my legs, so to speak, I went back to him and asked him if he still needed help, and he did. I learned in a couple of days, and it was a very interesting job. We were cleaning windows for Elvis Presley, Lucille Ball, and years later, I cleaned windows for Telly Savalas. How cool is that! I cleaned windows for the CEO of Scania-Vabis from Sweden. He had a big mansion in the Vintage Club in Indian Wells. I also cleaned windows for Walt Disney's home every month for 12 years until I sold my window cleaning company, and the new owner continued.

I had already realized that I wanted to stay in America. It was because of the American people. I had never met people who were so friendly and warm. So I called my mom and told her that I was going to make this my home.

"What do you mean? You're not coming home anymore?"

I told her how much I loved it here. However, when the nine-month visa ran out, I returned to Sweden to get rid of my apartment and my belongings. And while I was home, I remember driving through my old community, and when I passed the roundabout, I spotted a big guy walking down the highway. It was my old school friend Mats. I stopped and talked to him, and he said, "I heard you've been to America."

"Yes," I told him enthusiastically, "and I'm going back to stay." With a smile, I said, "You want to come?"

Immediately, he said, "Yes!!"

And I started laughing. I said, "You really made up your mind fast."

"Well, my sister lived in Chicago for many years. So I always wanted to go there after listening to her."

"Wow, that is great. So it looks like our road in life is gonna continue. I've known you since second grade."

I also invited my brother, Leif, my friend Kjell, and an old girlfriend, Vivi. I took action immediately, hired an immigration attorney, and started the immigration process for the United States. I thought it would be easier to do it in Sweden due to the language barrier I had in California. But when the time came to go back to the U.S., all my friends except me had received their visas in time for the flight. I finally found out why. It was because I had started to emigrate from Sweden, and I found out that I couldn't enter American soil before the immigration process was final. Unbelievably, I was told that it could take five years or even longer. Immediately, I contacted my attorney and told him that I had changed my mind. I had decided to stop the immigration papers.

However, in my mind, I figured it was probably easier to find a girl and get married when I got back to California. I had it all figured out! A couple of days before the flight was going to leave, I had still had not received my visa. I was not going to stay in Sweden, so I decided to go to Australia instead. That was too bad because my friend Kenny had already arranged a house that we would rent and live in. I told my friends it looked like they would have to go to California without me, but to my surprise, the day before the plane was leaving, I miraculously got my visa. I could finally join all my friends whom I'd invited to come back to California with me.

Two days later, the whole gang arrived in California. I had a six-month visa, and everything was good. I went back to window cleaning. We did some traveling and discovered all the beautiful things in California.

Well, as the saying goes, "Time flies when you're having fun." Soon, the six months were coming to an end, and my visa was about to expire. I said to Kenny, "Wow, time has gone by so fast, and I have to find a girl so I can get married. It's time to get a green card and a working permit." And only a week later, at our favorite nightclub, Jilly's, while sitting there looking, I spotted a girl and two guys coming in through the front entrance and sitting down at a table across the dance floor. She was the most beautiful gal I'd ever seen! I pointed her out to Kenny, and for some funny reason, I told Kenny, "I'm going to marry her." (I still can't believe that I said that!) As soon as they sat down at their table, I walked across the floor and asked the girl to dance.

To my surprise, she said yes! This nightclub had a live band playing every night, and after having been steady guests for close to a year, my friends and I were almost part of the inventory. We were very good friends with the guys in the band, Wayne and Frank. And now I was proceeding to dance with the most beautiful girl I had ever seen, and I didn't want to lose her. So you know what I did? I kept her occupied on the dance floor! We danced three dances, even though I didn't speak any English. It was very warm in there that night, and I noticed her hair was touching her face, and she was constantly blowing it out of the way. For some funny reason, I wanted to find a way to stop that hair from bothering her, so I started to blow in her face when we were dancing. And it looked like I'd solved the problem! Every time I did that, she laughed — so cute — so I kept doing it during the last two dances. Who would have thought to do such a thing? But it worked. Maybe she got drunk from my breath, LOL!

Finally, she indicated that she had to sit down. After all, she had two guys waiting for her. I figured they would be really upset by now, but I said to myself, *Bring it on*. I walked her back to her table, and the guys weren't very happy. After a while, I noticed they were ready to leave the place, and I quickly ran over and asked that cute gal for her phone number. It was the only thing I could say in English: "Telephone number." Pretty good. "Telephone" is the same in Swedish, and "number" is very close.

As quickly as possible, I gave her my pen and put my arm out, and she wrote the phone number on my arm. I felt like I had gone to heaven. I couldn't believe that she would do that. Wow. I was so happy I could fly! Now, I needed a translator, and of course, my buddy Kenny spoke fluent English. As a result, he had to call her every time I wanted to ask her out. A few short weeks later, I felt that I had to take the next step and ask her if she would marry me. If she said no, I'd have to start looking for somebody else because my visa was going to run out soon.

I'd done many wild and crazy things in my life, and I told Winnie upfront, "I am going to be honest with you. I need a green card so I can continue to live in America and work." I asked her, "Would you marry me?"

To my surprise, she said, "Yes, I will marry you!"

Wow, I could not have been happier! A couple of days later, on a Monday, I gave her $20 to go and buy a ring. I found out later it was not enough, and she had put down $20 herself. The following Tuesday afternoon, we went to a church in Palm Springs and got married. Our witnesses were my brother, Leif, my buddy Mats, Kjell, Kenny, and Vivi.

Winnie and me on our wedding day.

After the ceremony, we went home. Kenny's mom and dad were waiting for us when we came home, and they threw rice all over us. It was awesome! Soon thereafter, we rented our first apartment together at Landau Apartments in Palm Springs. After we moved in, I started to let my feelings open up to my new wife. You know how it is: when you don't really know if you're going to stay together, you don't want to leave your heart wide open. However, the more we were together, the more I could feel that we were really meant for one another. She was the nicest, sweetest person I'd ever met. Later, I would meet her son, James, who had been living with his father, and we became a family. In 2023, Winnie and I celebrated 50 years of marriage!

P.S. Soon after we got married, I asked Winnie about the day when she gave me her phone number, and she explained that she never gave guys her real phone number. When she met somebody new, she would always write down a different number. She never understood why she had given me the correct phone number right off the bat. However, 50 years later, I know God wanted it to be this way because I could never have found a better wife than my cute little Winnie!

I have been looking for photos to use in my book, and to my surprise, I found a letter at the bottom of a little wooden box that my beautiful wife wrote right after she came home from Moby's, which used to be called Jilly's. This is amazing, and it confirms exactly what I have been saying in my testimony. I will type exactly what it says in this letter. And you can even see a photo of her original copy below. Wow, I can hardly believe my eyes. This is what she wrote.

My life with Samuelsson

I met him October of 1972. I first met him at Moby's, at the dancing place in Palm Springs. I was with two of my Filipino friends. I was sitting at the table with my friends, having our drink. And in one corner of this place was another party of people. I could hear that they were loud. After a little while, this tall man came to our table to ask if I would like to dance. Since my friends were not interested to dance, I went and danced with this tall man. I was very surprised; he was blowing air into my face. We danced for a while. After a long while, I was thirsty. I went back to my table and had a drink. I had promised him a dance after my drink. When he came back, my friends were getting ready to go home. He came over to me and asked for my telephone number. I gave him a number. I really thought I gave him a wrong telephone number but later on, two days after, I got a call from him.

My Life with Samuelsson

I met him October of 1972
I first meet hem at mobys at
a Dancing plase in palm springs I
was with two of my phillipiño friends
I was setting at the Table with my
friend having our Drink. and in
one corner of this plase was
another party of peaple I could
hear that they ware loud after
a lettle whell this tall man
came to our table to ask if I
would like to dance. sence my
friends was not interested to
dance I went and Dance
with this tall man I was very
surprize he was Blowing air in
to my pace. we dance for a whell
after a long whell I was tersty
I went back to my Table and had
a drink I had promist hem a Dance
after my Drink. when he came back
my friends was getting ready leave
home he came over to me and ask for
my Telephone number. I gave hem a
number I realy Thaugh I gave hem
a phony Telephone number but
later on two days after I got
a call from hem

Winnie's letter about meeting me for the first time.

Our wedding day (Winnie and me in the middle).

I was still working for the window cleaner. One day, he told me Eisenhower Hospital wanted us to clean the windows, so we went there and looked at the buildings. They were three stories high, and he said, "This is too high. There's no way we can clean that high up."

But I told him, "Let's buy a long extension ladder, and I'll do all the high windows outside." It was a huge job because it was two buildings. Well, he got the job and purchased a very long extension ladder that was over 40 feet long. When I got up there to the top of the ladder, it was amazing how narrow the extension ladder looked at the bottom when you're up on the third floor. Before we started this project, my boss promised me he would pay me half of the profits because I was climbing so high. Unfortunately, when I went to get paid, I believe he changed his mind, and I only got the regular pay, $0.50 an hour!

I've always been honest and because of this, I told him I could not work for him anymore and walked out of his house.

Amazingly, a week later, he handed over a group of apartment buildings to me. And I was very grateful for that; those apartments were very time-consuming to clean. They had eight louvered windows in each kitchen, and it was very difficult to make a profit. Later on, I had to find a way to reduce the labor. That's when I invented my first window cleaning tool, the Tricket louver window cleaning tong, which I will discuss a little bit later in my book.

Unfortunately, this was the only account I had at that time. I didn't have enough work to make a living, so I started to work part-time for a Swedish carpenter. His name was Kenneth Wilhelmsson. During that time, I learned a lot about building homes: everything from digging footings to framing, painting, masonry work, electrical work, building brick walls, installing Formica on countertops in kitchens, and all kinds of finishing work. It was a very exciting time. It wasn't too long after this that the customers belonging to the window cleaning company I'd previously worked for started calling me and asking if I could come and clean their windows. They said they had been trying to find me. Many more customers called me, and all of a sudden, the window cleaning business started to grow by leaps and bounds. And my boss, Kenneth, encouraged me to build up the window cleaning business. I started to fill out the workweek with window cleaning accounts.

Cleaning windows in the '70s, at the beginning of my career.

1973: Gambling in Las Vegas

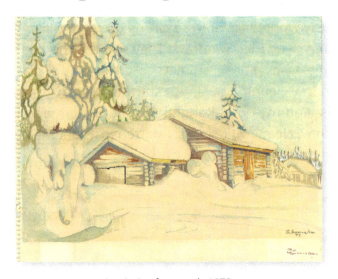

A painting from early 1973.

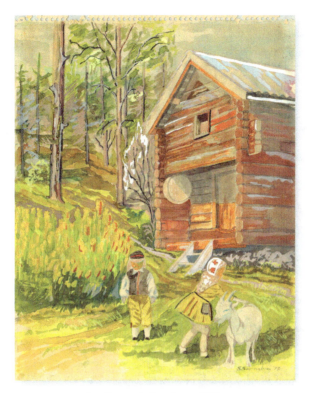

Another painting from 1973.

My Swedish friends visiting America.

Me and my friends Kenny and Vivi, having some drinks.

My first chopper in the late '70s.

My window cleaning business was growing, and I was working out of my car. I had been trying to save enough money to buy a second vehicle, and I was really looking for a van. However, in those days most of my money went into my cars! So it seemed like I never had enough money. My old school buddy Mats, our wives, and a few more buddies used to go to Las Vegas once a year to gamble. I had never been a big gambler, but I played keno, which was a pretty simple game. I didn't believe I would win any money, so I always played for the lowest amount, 65 cents. Just for fun. We always set a $100 limit. That's why I decided to play for the lowest amount, so it would last longer.

We took the elevator down to the casino floor, and to my surprise, the first game I played, I won $1,100. Some of my buddies screamed, "Let's party — you pay for the drinks!"

I said, "There is no way I'm going to buy drinks. I am going to buy a van for my window cleaning business." Consequently, I decided to play one more game, and then I was going to quit. The next game, I won $200. I could not believe it! I stopped right there, and I didn't play anymore.

1973: Almost Like New

When I returned to Palm Springs, I started to look for a used van. After looking at a few of them, I realized that most weren't in good shape considering the price, and if they were, I couldn't afford them. About the same time, I saw an ad in the paper. A local liquor store in Palm Springs had a 1969 half-ton Chevy van with a 208 cubic inch V8 listed for $1,500. I knew there had to be something wrong with it for that price. I called them up right away to talk to the owner. Sure enough, he told me that there was something wrong with the engine. I knew that whatever was wrong, I could fix it because I used to work with

V8 engines. I knew I could fix it because they are pretty easy to work on.

Well, I went over there, I took it for a ride, and I realized that it was running on only seven cylinders, so I offered him what I had, $1,000, and he said yes! The van was in excellent condition. The only thing that I could complain about was that it needed a wax job. It was bright yellow, but it looked like it had never been waxed because it was oxidized. Much later, I waxed it, and it looked brand new. Again, I checked the spark plugs, and I noticed right away that one of the spark plugs was very hard to get to, and it had never been changed. Install a new plug, and the car would run like new. I called the owner of the liquor store and told him. He was grateful, and then he told me he was going to look for a new service company.

Cleaning windows at the La Quinta Country Club when it first opened.

In 1973, my wonderful wife and I decided to take a long trip across the country, and go up to New York to visit my aunt and uncle.

Custom vans were a new, popular trend in the '70s. The one I had was a good example of that. I built a nice bed in the back and a bar in the middle of it. Away we went to do some sightseeing for two months' vacation on the way up to Catskill, New York, where my aunt and uncle lived. My uncle was working for the Kingston factory in upstate New York. Winnie and I got jobs there, where we worked for two months. They had one department that made things for accessible bathrooms, and with my welding background, I was welding stainless steel tubing for the handrails that go onto the wall beside a toilet. I realized that the people who had worked there for many years were extremely slow. I welded easily twice as many products as other welders completed. My wife did the same thing in her department. The other workers didn't like it and, as a result, they more or less became very unfriendly with my wife and me. It got so bad that they didn't even talk to us when we were clocking out. It didn't bother me because I dislike lazy people.

My uncle was a foreman, and he was very proud of us. I got four pay increases during those two months! It was unheard of. When the time came for us to continue traveling, the leadership begged us to stay and work for the company! We had a good time showing the people how to work efficiently, but we had to keep on going toward Portland, Oregon, to visit my wife's aunt, Auntie Anita. Following our visit, we continued down to Palm Springs. It was a summer we will never forget.

1974: DeVille Collision

A year later, I would have my first car accident in America. One evening, we were driving home from Mats and Rosita's. We were driving through Palm Springs on Highway 111 when, all of a sudden, a big Cadillac DeVille didn't stop at the stop sign on a cross street. At full speed, it drove into the driver's door of my van and pushed it into the curb, which was 7 inches high, extremely high. We then continued moving in between two palm trees, and my van kept turning left. We ended up in the middle of the street, facing in the opposite direction. Immediately, I looked at my wife and saw that her entire face was swollen up like a football. I don't know where all the blood came from. Her whole face was totally black, and her eyes were sunk deep into that distorted face.

My '69 Chevy van after the accident.

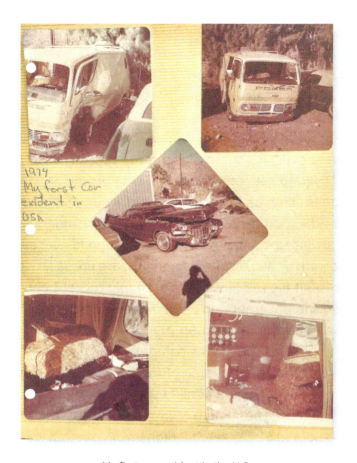

My first car accident in the U.S.

"Oh honey, are you okay?"

"I don't know," she said, and by that time, there were people surrounding our vehicle, and an ambulance had come.

I was released from the hospital that night, but my wife had to stay there because she could not even see. Her face was swollen, and we found out later on that one of the nurses, who was an old friend of hers, hadn't even recognized her. The doctor had to suck all the blood out of her swollen skull, and she lost two of her front teeth.

That was the first time I was in an accident, and it wasn't my fault. After a couple of days, Winnie was released, and she went to the dentist to get new teeth implants. But now, our '69 Chevy van was totaled, so I purchased a Dodge van, and I fixed it up the same way.

A couple of years later, Winnie, Mindi, Kenny's dad, Stig, and I went over the mountains in Anza, California, and down to San Diego to get some products. On the way back home, it was a steep climb up toward Anza, and around 500 feet up the highway, the road curved to the right. All of a sudden, we saw a big car driving up on the mountainside. It tipped over and came down toward us at full speed, spinning like a propeller, traveling on its roof. It looked like a Fourth of July rocket between the roof and the pavement. I realized I couldn't get off the road because I had a mountain on my right-hand side, so I drew in to the right as much as I could, in the hope that the car would keep sliding on its side of the road. It came closer and closer, not slowing down at all because it was going downhill, and I thought, *Maybe if I step on the gas, I can pass it when the car is at 12 o'clock to 6 o'clock*, but it didn't work out that way. There was a tremendous crash, and the trunk of the car hit me right in front of my passenger seat. When you look at the previous accident with my '69 Chevrolet van, the damage was just about in the same place: very strange — right over my legs.

It was a good thing that Winnie and Mindi were sleeping on the floor in the back of the van, and they didn't really know what was happening, but Stig, my passenger, was sitting in the front. He got shaken up pretty good, and when I asked if he was okay, he complained about his neck hurting. The other car kept turning the other way after the collision and continued down the highway 100 feet, and then it stopped. All of a sudden, it started to smoke inside my van, and Stig said, "It's a fire. Let's get out of here!"

It was coming from underneath the hood, that is, in between the seats in the front, and because I had the dashboard up against my chest from the impact, I didn't see that the hood over the engine in between the seats had come off. I actually saw the street right in front of me because the windows were gone. When I finally found out what was smoking, I realized it was my foot; it was stuck in between the headers on the engine and the floorboard. I didn't feel anything, so I finally got my foot out, and we looked at it. We could see that the bone was exposed, and the flesh was totally gone. It was evening before the ambulance came, and it was dark already, so they took us to the closest hospital in Escondido.

I got to meet some of the people who had been in the other car. They were Native Americans, three guys and two girls. I saw one of the guys lying on the table, and you could see his back was broken, sticking out of his shirt. I found out later that he had died soon after that.

We were released from the hospital the following day, so they told me to go to my local hospital when I got home, but I didn't. I was jumping around on crutches for one week. I thought my foot would heal by itself, but all of a sudden, it started to hurt, and I had to go to Indio Community Hospital (later renamed John F. Kennedy (JFK) Hospital). The doctor told me that it was a good thing I went in because the flesh was so infected. They ended up doing a big scraping job to remove half-rotten flesh, and then they did a skin graft, so I ended up staying there for a few days. It doesn't really pay to be stubborn.

I ended up purchasing another van for the business, so everything worked out fine.

1974: Purchasing a 1969 Shelby GT500 Mustang 429 Cobra

My Shelby Cobra, as well as my Mustang, at my first apartment.

In 1972, I purchased a Mustang Mark 1, but a year before I left Sweden, I had looked at a '68 Shelby Cobra. After that, I wanted to buy a Ford Shelby Cobra car one day, and finally, in 1974, I saved up enough money. Because of the oil crisis that year, many people wanted to get rid of their big engines, so I put an ad in the *Los Angeles Times*: Shelby Cobra wanted. Three Cobra owners contacted me. One of them had a 1969 Shelby GT500 King of the Road convertible with a big 429 cubic inch block in it.

I went to LA right away and purchased that car. The first thing I did was to take the engine out and build some more horsepower into it. I totally rebuilt it, added a Holley double pumper on it and a sharper cam, and then I took it to the Orange County Raceway and dragged it a couple of times, originally doing a quarter-mile in 16 seconds. I improved and got it down to 12 seconds.

My love for cars and building engines is still going on; right now, I am building my biggest engine, a 632-inch stroker (which I will tell you more about later on in this book).

In 1974, I became an American citizen. I had the opportunity to vote for President Reagan, and that was a happy moment in my life. I did not have much time for my family in between inventing and working. I've never been to any of my daughters' events. My wife did all of that herself. I am so grateful for her. Through the years, most of the money I made went to equipment and patents, and we had very little to live on, but my wife was a fantastic person to handle the financial part of our business and family life. I continue to develop equipment.

1974: Hard Choices

After three years, I had less time for carpentry work, so I quit working as a carpenter. Window cleaning is seasonal down here in the desert, and I had some spare time in the summer. I got a job working for another Swedish guy, remodeling a big hotel across from Disneyland in Anaheim. His name was Frank Jagarius and we got to talking about where he'd lived in Sweden and where his home was because he came from outside Östersund where I was stationed in the army.

My new 1969 Shelby Cobra.

Another accident in my '74 Dodge van.

I told him the story I told you earlier in this book about me crashing my car, and to my surprise, it was his mom and dad I was talking to in that little house so many years earlier. And his Swedish last name was Anderson; he changed it when he came to America. Remember, I thought I was lying to the taxi driver when I came up with a name. Now, more than ten years later, I find out that I didn't lie; their name actually was Anderson. It's amazing. It's a small world.

We did a lot of fire jobs for insurance companies. We were four guys working together, and all of us liked to drink beer. We would start to drink at around 9 o'clock in the morning, and in the evening, sometimes we ended up in the bars in downtown Palm Springs. This is how life went on, but everybody worked every day, not staying home.

In 1974, I was still doing window cleaning, but on the days when I did window cleaning, I was not drinking; I only drank in the evenings. After a few years, I got so many window-cleaning customers that I had to quit my job as a carpenter and start to clean windows full-time. I knew that I could not drink during the day anymore, but I also realized that I could not kick the habit of drinking, so my drinking became a nightly activity. I was working through the days, sometimes with a hangover. It was very difficult when I grew older. I had never tried to quit drinking before, but now, when I wanted to quit, I realized that I could not, and it became a personal nightmare. I felt so depressed and sick about myself. I could hold out for a day or two sometimes, but I always fell back, and I felt really bad about it. I got so tired of it that I was thinking about ending my life, and I even went to a gun shop and ordered a gun. The owner handed me a book to read while I was waiting for the gun permit, and in it, I read that people who purchased guns sometimes woke up in the middle of the night and, by mistake, killed their own wives. I was thinking *That could be me; that could happen to me*, so I canceled the order.

1975: Perfecting for a Patent

As mentioned earlier, I invented the Tricket, the louvered window-cleaning tongue, but didn't apply for a patent for it until 1984. When I quit working for my old boss, perhaps out of guilt, he provided me with work by way of 200 apartments that he owned, each with eight louvered kitchen windows. It was very difficult to make a good profit, so I invented a new tool that I later called the Tricket. Before that, it was very time-consuming because we had to clean each side of the window panels with the squeegee. The idea came to me to make tongs from the brass squeegee so I could clean both sides at the same time. Therefore, I took a standard brass squeegee and bent it into a U-shape, and it worked. My first invention was born! Later, I started to make a prototype and came to a final design. As a result, I could do the windows in one-third of the time!

A few years later, I didn't think that much about it. I had just made the tongs to make my job easier and increase my profit. Some customers from Hawaii were looking through their window at my tongs. This was their second home, and they said, "We should have these tongs in Hawaii because all the homes over there have louvered windows. It is their form of a heating and cooling system."

I started to be a little worried about my invention. Consequently, I started to work on a better design so I could patent it, and it wasn't long before I had a perfect design! I made it in stainless steel and inserted two 6-inch squeegee blades to match the glass panels. You can insert longer squeegees if needed. The Tricket was also adjustable for different thicknesses of glass: by unscrewing the wing nut on the left side, you can easily change that. In 1984, it became a big seller! Of course, here in America, louvered windows were slowly disappearing. But we still had a lot of vertical blinds, wooden shutters, and glass bar shelves. At that time, we still had to wash the windows with a sponge, but soon after, I developed the second set of Tricket with sponge pads so you could wash both sides at the same time. The sponge pads were later changed to the Yellow Jacket washer sleeves that hold a lot more water without dripping. Finally, I had developed a totally new concept of cleaning louvered windows, and those apartments became extremely profitable! There was even a window cleaning company in Hawaii that sold a large number of Trickets over there. They showed a really nice TV commercial one Christmas, so I think many Hawaiians have benefited from this tool.

My Tricket prototype in 1973 (my first invention).

1976: Purchasing Our Own Home

Our garage-based factory in our first house.

Making my first invention in the garage

We didn't have much money, but I had two cars. I had a 1970 Ford van, which I did some custom work on. Later on, it was shown in a couple of hot rod magazines. In those days, it was popular to build a bar in the middle of the van and also to have a bed in the back of it. I also had a 1969 Shelby GT500 King of the Road convertible. That's all we had to our name in 1975!

We had an apartment, but I was planning to take those two cars to Sweden in 1976 and sell them. My wife was pregnant with Mindi, and we needed a home, and this would be the money for the down payment. We stayed in Sweden for three months. I worked for two months at my old job as a mechanic and welder. With the money I received from working and selling the two cars, we saved up enough money, so when we came back to California, we were able to purchase a home in Palm Desert, which we still own to this day! Through the years, I have done a lot of remodeling. I built a pool myself and remodeled the whole house.

Through the years, when we were cleaning windows, I got to know David and Kay, a wonderful couple who worked in the office at one country club where we used to pick up the keys for the homes we were cleaning windows in. I asked Kay if she would work for us when she retired, and she said yes. Kay became a very important part of our business because she could do all the bookkeeping and invoices, as well as all the communication letters that needed to be done.

And later, our house became our first factory when we started to market our Sörbo Products! The garage was where I cut all the channels, and we used the rest of the house for packaging and the office. My wife and I were discussing a name for our company, and Winnie, being ever so clever, came up with a suggestion. "Why don't you use half of your first name and your middle name?" She said, "Use SÖR from your first name, Sören, and BO from your middle name, and it will be SÖRBO." Little did she know that there were many places in Sweden named Sörbo. However, I thought it was a great idea with the umlaut over the Ö. It would be a cool name, and Sörbo Products was born! Later on, I incorporated all the letters in Sörbo into the artwork that I designed, with the round ring in the center with two eyes up above. If you look at that, you can see all the letters S>O>R>B>O>in it.

My first invention was the Tricket, patent number 4,468,833, and it was registered on September 4, 1984.

Winnie and I eating pizza together in November 1977.

Winnie (right), her friend, and me in the middle, with my Caddy.

My Caddy and me.

Part III
My Innovation Begins

1984: The Docket. Patent Number 4,604,802

My second invention, the Docket, in 1984.

My second invention was the Docket. It was 1984, and at that time, we had the world oil crisis that was bringing all the gas prices up. Everybody was talking about finding new ways of saving energy and reducing the waste of petroleum products. As I was changing my squeegee blade at the end of the day at one of my customer's worksites, which I did every day, I said *this is petroleum-made*, and that's when the idea came to me. If I could sharpen the rubber instead of throwing it away every night, I would have a lot less waste. At that moment, the idea for the first squeegee rubber sharpener in the world was born! I was thinking how much money window cleaners would save if this worked.

I went home that evening, and I put the squeegee rubber between two pieces of angle iron and clamped them together with two vice grips. And then, I took a razor blade and tried to slide it across and remove the worn-out portion of the squeegee rubber. Unfortunately, it did not work very well at all. I said to myself, *This is a tremendous idea. I have to make it work*. I knew I had to use a very precise tool to get the same thickness from one end to the other on a 36-inch squeegee rubber. Thankfully, when I invent something, I have a writing pad beside my bed, and many times during the night, problems are solved, and I write it down! There are some nights when I even happen to go out into the garage and work on something in the middle of the night because it's always so exciting when you finally overcome an obstacle. I knew this would be the greatest invention I had created to date.

A year and a half later, I had finally developed the first squeegee rubber sharpener in the world that worked perfectly!! I named it the Docket. In the beginning, I made three sizes: 18-inch, 24-inch, and 36-inch. Later on, I realized that you can sharpen any size in the 36-inch Docket, so I eliminated the other two sizes.

1984: Invention #3, the First Wide-Body Aluminum Squeegee, Patented, September 16, 1985

Sörbo's Black Mamba, the first Sörbo 3 x 4 Adjustable Wide-Body squeegee. Invented in 1984 and patented in 1985. This features the white squeegee rubber invented in 1994.

In 1984, I invented the first 36-inch Wide-Body squeegee in the world. I named it Sörbo 3 × 4 Adjustable Wide-Body squeegee. It was made from high-quality aircraft aluminum and was the first jet-black squeegee ever made. Historically, it's the only squeegee that has two separate patents. It's now 47 years later, and today, the Sörbo Adjustable Wide-Body squeegee is the most duplicated squeegee in history. Every manufacturing company is making wide-body squeegees!! I appreciate that they respect my original wide-body squeegee designs. Sörbo Products has a record-breaking nine different models. The other companies on the market all have their own separate designs, so you can recognize which company made each specific wide-body squeegee.

Amazingly, the window cleaning industry was very dull when I started to clean windows. There were only a few colors: brass, stainless, black ABS plastic, and leather. However, in those days, window cleaning was not an extremely attractive profession! It was not uncommon to see a bum walking around with a paint bucket, a squeegee, and a washer just to make enough money for a six-pack of beer. Accordingly, I said to myself, *What the industry needs is some new innovative products with a plethora of new colors*. We'd never had a squeegee over 24 inches, so the first squeegee I made was the 36-inch Black Mamba. I also came up with the first colored squeegee rubber in white, and I was the first one to develop a softer rubber, which was designed for the wide-body squeegee. With that technology and special angles, the new squeegee would close off the stroke against the frame without leaving water, so Sörbo was 30 years ahead in manufacturing one soft and one harder rubber.

I started to get very excited about developing revolutionary new equipment. This was due to antiquated equipment being used in the window cleaning industry. Can you imagine all the other industries using electric equipment like circular saws for the carpenter, instead of handsaws? Here we were in the 1970s and we were still using the same squeegee that was invented in 1936!!

That was when an immigrant from Italy invented and patented a totally new design where you could slide the squeegee rubber into the channel and secure it with two end clips. The squeegees that had been used before that were called the Chicago squeegee: a very simple squeegee made in the shape of a flat metal bar with a handle attached and a multitude of holes. You actually attached a couple of flat rubber strips in between the two flat bars and tightened the screws and nuts.

However, in the 1970s, another window cleaner entered the American market and introduced the same squeegee in stainless steel. THK made a stainless steel squeegee with a two-sided squeegee rubber. They also attached the squeegee and the washer together in one unit. Just turn the washer over and use the squeegee. By the way, that company disappeared from the market a few years later.

I always wanted a bigger squeegee so I could reduce labor. This particular squeegee was not made rigid enough to be longer. The brass channels were made in sizes up to 22 inches, and the stainless steel squeegee went up to 24 inches, but in order to use that squeegee, you had to bend it like a bow. As a result, you achieved more pressure at each end, and that is the way I use that squeegee. The downside was that the rubber wore out close to the ends really quickly because of the increased pressure. You wasted more rubber, but that didn't matter when you could clean windows faster. I was still changing rubber every day in my squeegees. One window cleaner dog-eared the channels at each end, but that actually wore the squeegee rubber out even quicker, so I never did that. What was needed was a totally new squeegee that would not bend at all.

Nevertheless, I realized that once you have invented a product, all of a sudden, it opens up new avenues for another invention as a result of the one you just invented. It's like a chain reaction. It seems like each of the products I invented over the years had a connection to the products I had invented before that. That's what happened with the adjustable wide-body squeegee: because of the Docket that I invented in 1974, in 2024, it is still the only squeegee rubber sharpener in the world. I realized that, with the present squeegees, you could only sharpen the squeegee blade once, and if you sharpened it one more time you'd start to clean the window with the metal channel instead of the rubber, LOL. That's not good! I also knew that people would not pay that much money for a squeegee blade sharpener if they could only sharpen the rubber once. So, I wanted to invent a squeegee where you could sharpen the rubber as many times as possible, and that is why I designed the Sörbo 3 × 4 to be T-shaped rubber instead of round. By making it T-shaped, I had room for four adjustments, so you could sharpen the squeegee rubber three times in each adjustment. That's how it got its name. I called it 3 × 4 because it equals 12 possible sharpenings. With this design, you can also adjust the firmness of the rubber itself. By sliding the rubber out and moving it out one step, you make the rubber softer, and by moving it in, you increase the firmness. I also came up with a center mark in the channel so the window cleaner can see where the center is. I came up with four different designs, and I made the first prototype squeegee design out of hardwood. I always make the prototypes first to get the right design, and then I would go to the drawing board and make blueprints.

When I was satisfied with this revolutionary new design, I contacted an extrusion company and made the first aircraft aluminum squeegee in the world. As soon as I got the first copy made, I tried it, and I was amazed at how well it performed; it needed very light pressure. I also wanted this to be the highest standard of squeegee on the market, and instead of printing the name on the channel itself, I developed the label that we insert in the channel with the size in both inches and metric so the window cleaner can tell right away what size it is.

More window cleaning, from 1985.

I had to figure out how to keep the label in the channel. I knew that using some kind of glue would be too time-consuming, but I kept thinking about it with my writing pad beside my bed during the night. I woke up one night with the idea to make a special press that would squeeze the channel together as a means of holding the label in place. And that became the first squeegee with the center mark in the middle of the channel.

Going back a few years, I knew that window cleaning was very hard work, and I started to study how much energy was needed to clean windows with the existing technique — the slalom method, or the "fanning" method, as we called it! I also realized that window cleaners developed pain in the wrists, elbows, and shoulders. During the '80s, I had a hard time finding window cleaners who had mastered the skilled technique of fanning a window. Consequently, I advertised for help in Sweden. The first guy who came over to work for me lasted only a month due to an old injury he had in his shoulder. Unfortunately, we ended up taking him to the hospital here, and then he returned to Sweden. But then, my uncle and his friend Konrad, the owner of Moskogen in Leksand, Sweden, visited me, and he told me about another window cleaner, Tommy Södergren. So I gave Tommy a call and asked if he would like to come to California and clean windows. He said, "I'll be there next week."

And he became the best employee I ever had. You can set a clock by this guy. He's never sick and has worked for me for eight years. I'll tell you later in the book what happened to him. Thus, I decided to change things through the years. I've hired many people who were not able to do the fanning method. They just didn't have the skill. Very few people were able to do it because it was an art.

I remember, one week, I hired and fired five people. I started teaching them in the morning, and after eight hours, you could tell if they were going to be a window cleaner or not. Most of them never passed the test! This is something that I had in mind when I started to design my new wide-body squeegee channel. If I didn't have to teach the fanning method anymore, that would help build the business. I have never seen anyone who cannot do three horizontal strokes with the new Sörbo 36-inch 3 × 4 adjustable wide-body squeegee on a sliding glass door.

However, as a direct result of my new techniques, I could hire anyone, and they were able to do the windows as fast as the guys who were fanning the windows! This took only one-third of the effort as well as the time, and that opened up the doors for more window cleaning companies. So, I developed the most rigid channel anyone had ever seen, and it was still extraordinarily lightweight. It was also the largest squeegee in the world! I realized that with a special new design, my channel was more rigid. I started out with the 36-inch, and a few years later, the 48-inch, up to the 78-inch Eliminator. This new design reduced two-thirds of the labor when you cleaned a sliding glass window. Instead of crossing the window back and forth and going over the dry surface in the traditional slalom technique, or what some people call the "fanning" technique, you could move your hand around 28 to 32 feet on each sliding glass door! Think about that. I realized that if you did 200 windows a day, you would move your arm around 6,000 feet a day with an 18-inch squeegee. If you used a 36-inch squeegee and did three horizontal passes, you would move your arm only 10 feet for each window. That, times 200, is 2,000 feet! That's incredible!

As a result, you reduce movement by two-thirds. That got me thinking, and I never looked back. Ten years later, I received the second patent for the Sörbo 3 × 4 adjustable wide-body Cobra channel with the safety end plugs. Mr. Sörbo is the only window cleaner who has two separate patents on squeegees! If you look at my ad from 1986, which I drew by hand in those days, it says, "Tomorrow's squeegee, here today." Currently, today my Sörbo 3 × 4 Adjustable Wide-Body squeegee is the most duplicated squeegee in history. Every manufacturing company is making our wide-body squeegees.

In addition, on YouTube, you can view window cleaners demonstrating the techniques that I invented: the Z method, the upside-down L method that my wife developed, and the fastest method of them all — the upside-down U method. Also, on YouTube, you can see a film from 1980 where I am in a race with another window cleaner. He managed to do two passes by the time I was done with the whole window. Then, of course, there is the reverse stroke, where you can go back and forth with the 36-inch squeegee without taking the squeegee off the window. And that is because, with my new design, you can go up against the frame and finish the stroke without leaving any water at all.

In August 1986, the first *American Window Cleaner Magazine* was delivered to my mailbox. Our employees had now been using our squeegees for close to two years, and we all knew that we could do the windows so much faster with the new Sörbo 3 × 4 adjustable wide-body squeegee.

We even lost one of our customers because we finished their house a lot quicker than before. It was a monthly account, and I personally never met the owner! He was the owner of a big trucking company, and he had several homes. Every time we went to his mansion, the housekeeper opened up the house. But because we were so much faster with our new 36-inch Sörbo 3 × 4 Adjustable Wide-Body squeegee, the housekeeper thought we were skipping windows. She obviously called the owner and told him that we'd cheated on the job. He believed her, and as a result, we lost that account. It didn't really matter that much because we had a few people waiting for our service. Consequently, my wife and I started to talk about marketing our product, but we didn't know where to start. I didn't have any experience in marketing or manufacturing. I just happened to be a window cleaner who had come up with a few new inventions. On the positive side, we increased our income quite a bit by using this new equipment, so it was time to start selling it to the window cleaning industry.

As I said before, amazingly, wouldn't you know it, the following week, the first issue of *American Window Cleaner Magazine* showed up in our mailbox!! I started reading the Publishers' Corner. The magazine was founded by two guys, Richard Fabry and Rod Woodward. This couldn't have happened at a better time for our new company! I immediately called Rod and Richard, and we had a long talk. Rod explained to me the process of his swivel handle invention. We also discussed the Black Mamba. He got so excited about a black squeegee. The next week, I visited them at their headquarters in Berkeley, California, with a group of other people. It was a fantastic experience meeting the crew who had got the window cleaning world together for the first time and — even more significant — it was the most important outlet for exposing my inventions to the window cleaning industry. For the first time, I got to know window cleaners from all over the country, and of course, nowadays, Mr. "Jersey" Josh Cronin has increased the *AWC Magazine* distribution worldwide.

On March 14, 1987, I was invited to a window cleaning seminar in San Jose, California, where I met a handful of professional window cleaners. One of them was Mark Heckler. He realized that my products had potential and purchased the first 36-inch Sörbo 3 × 4 Adjustable Wide-Body squeegee. Mark was the first outsider, besides our employees, to use our products.

Winnie and I getting ready to go to the next customer.

Invanted 1986 89

The original logo for Sörbo that I designed in 1986. I drew this
by hand to show how all the letters fit into the symbol.

The final product of my design!

1987: The First Annual Southwest Window Cleaning Workshop and Safety Seminar, Lubbock, Texas

A newsletter featuring a group of us from the Southwest window cleaning seminar in Lubbock (lower right).

Standing with the founders of AWC Magazine.

The seminar was arranged by Jim and Jacinda Willingham at the Paragon Hotel in Lubbock. It was an exciting time. We had already introduced the Tricket and the Docket Sörbo 3 × 4 Adjustable Wide-Body squeegee in black, and the high bucket stand, the Quatropod. This event gave birth to the International Window Cleaning Association (IWCA) two years later in Florida, but this is where the pioneer window cleaners met for the first time. We met the group of people who had been in the American window cleaning magazine. I am so proud that Sörbo was the only window-cleaning manufacturer present at this first event. We had the opportunity to meet some well-known window cleaners, including Jim and Jacinda Willingham of New

Day Window Cleaning; Rod Woodward and Richard Fabry, publishers of *AWC Magazine*; the owners of Jack Fitch Enterprises and Keifer Alpine Adventures, and many more. Rod Woodward demonstrated rappeling from the third floor to the lobby, and many of the attendees tried rappeling for the first time in their lives, including my brave wife, Winnie. She really loved it.

1987: An Early Marketing Strategy

I kept thinking about how to plan for my future as a manufacturing company. I knew early on when I started to invent new high-tech window cleaning equipment, that I could not afford to get into a price war with the other manufacturers who had much deeper pockets than this newcomer who had only his business to support him. I had a feeling this would be a product line strictly made for professional window cleaners — totally new high-tech equipment that homeowners would not pay for. Also, we decided to be 100 percent made in America and not to do what our competition did later on: have everything made in China. I love America, and this was going to be the only American-made squeegee line. This is why we are proud to make an American custom squeegee with stars and a red background, which has become so popular. And when you look at the pricing today for the wide-body squeegees, our squeegee is not among the most expensive ones. That is because I invented so many different time-saving pieces of equipment to manufacture our squeegees, so you can purchase the highest quality squeegee and the original wide-body squeegee for a more reasonable price. That is smart marketing, and that is why we sell a ton of squeegees today.

1987: My First Rubber Mold

Our press for our first 36-inch rubber mold.

Working hard in the garage factory!

A day in the life, cleaning more windows.

By this time, we needed more capital. I met with the loan officer at our bank and asked if he could get us a loan for the rubber mold that cost $40,000. I told the banker about my new invention and that we needed the loan to produce the 36-inch squeegee that I had invented. However, they were not too excited about it, and unfortunately, they could not give us the loan. Luckily, thanks be to God, my sister-in-law and her husband were willing to lend us the $40,000 for a mold. They believed our company would be a successful business.

I started cutting squeegee channels in our garage. I decided to make the first white squeegee rubber on the market. I made one soft and one hard; both were white. The reason I did that was because the rubber we were using for our squeegees many years back left black markings around the mirror where there was wallpaper. This happened in every home, around the bathroom mirrors. We realized later it was because of too much carbon in the rubber. Carbon is a filler, and it makes the squeegee glide better on the window, but it also reduces the durability, and the rubber wears out more quickly. I remembered this predicament, so I decided to make a squeegee rubber that wouldn't leave any marks. For this reason, the rubber didn't glide as easily on the window, but it held up forever. To compensate, we developed the Glide, which is the friction reducer. This product allows the squeegee to glide more easily, so you get the lubrication you need instead of having carbon in the squeegee rubber.

1987: Invention #5: The Quatropod. Patented, November 10, 1987

I developed serious back problems. I was still running my window cleaning business, and my wife had her own cleaning business. Over a period of time, I pinched a nerve in my lower back. At times, I had a chiropractor, who was very good, immediately readjust my sore back. Every time I walked out of his office, I walked straight. He was amazing; however, that summer, he was on vacation. Therefore, I had to find a different chiropractor. This new one made matters worse, and I became bedridden with extreme pain! Even though Winnie had her own house cleaning business, when I injured my back, she offered to work instead of me. She closed her cleaning company and started to clean windows with the guys, and she's only 5 foot 2.

Thankfully, because of the 36-inch Sörbo 3 × 4 Adjustable Wide-Body squeegee, she was able to reach the top of the windows. She is so awesome! All the years we've had together don't seem that long. I don't know where the time went! Well, I was lying there in bed, trying to figure out what was causing my problem. Then it hit me: I realized that I had been stooping all the way down to my bucket over 500 times a day for 16 years! As a result, that is when my fifth invention was born. I realized that the bucket had to come up to my hip height in order to reduce this exhausting maneuver. Nevertheless, I didn't really know what it should look like because when you work inside and between furniture, you can't have anything too wide. Sometimes, the squeegee holster gets stuck on something. This time, I didn't recover very fast. I actually ended up walking on crutches. The way this new chiropractor messed up my back, I ended up in the hospital and couldn't work for over a year. Finally, I recovered and went back to work, and it was really awesome to work with my wife.

Interestingly enough, one day, when we were cleaning a customer's windows, I spotted a flower stand in the living room that had three legs. I said, "This is it." I designed a bucket stand with three automatic folding legs and one kicker leg in the middle. When you lowered the bucket stand, the legs would fold outward to provide a sturdy base for the bucket. When you lifted up the bucket, all the legs collapsed toward the center leg and gave you great mobility for walking in between furniture and tight places. Finally, I came up with a name for this incredible back-saving product. I called it the Quatropod because it had four legs. It became an excellent workstation for all your tools.

It gave you flexibility, so you were freed from carrying a lot of things around on your belt.

I was still developing many new equipment ideas, and my employees and I really enjoyed working with these new tools that I had developed. Around this time, I had not marketed any of my inventions because I wanted to try them out with the window cleaning companies first. In order to get the bucket up as high as possible when you walk around with it, I put a handlebar inside the bucket and designed a mechanical tightening steel ring on the outside. To be honest, I wasn't very happy with the tightening steel ring because, after a while, the bucket contracted, and the stand fell off. Thankfully, I was discussing it with my wife, and she came up with the idea of a sliding lock device. As a result, I was able to design the two wings and the sliding locks. I'm so grateful to her for coming up with that clever idea; it became a great part of the bucket stand.

1987: The First ISSA Trade Show

In 1987, I decided to attend the International Sanitary Supply Association (ISSA) cleaning convention show in Houston. We needed to establish distributors for our products. At that time, we did not have a lot of capital, but we scraped enough money together for an airline ticket. I was there for only two days. I walked around the convention floor with a bucket stand in my briefcase as well as a Tricket and a Sörbo 3 × 4 Adjustable Wide-Body squeegee. I stopped and pitched my products to whoever would listen to me. I talked to different companies in their booths, and I picked up a lot of interest. I was very excited!! I had a stack of business cards that was a quarter-inch high, and they all wanted me to call them the following week regarding our product line.

The last night I was there, I went to my hotel room and went to sleep. In the morning, I woke up and found that somebody had been in my hotel room and stolen my briefcase, my airline tickets, and worst of all, my stack of business cards and my camera. I lost everything I had gathered during the show. I had to call my wife and tell her the bad news that I'd been robbed in my hotel room. Since I didn't have anything left — no money, no nothing —I asked her to buy me a new ticket. It took a whole year before I had the opportunity to go to the next show, and that was in New York City.

1988: Inventing the First 40-Foot Monster Pole

It was now 1988. Sörbo continued inventing new tools and astounding the window-cleaning world! The latest invention was the first 40-foot extension pole for window squeegees. This new invention of the extension pole was born because of the Sörbo 3 × 4 Adjustable Wide-Body squeegee I had invented a few years earlier. Since the rubber could be adjusted to different degrees of firmness, I realized that the squeegee could clean windows higher than any other squeegee in the world. However, I wanted to make the first 40-foot pole the window-cleaning world had ever seen. I came up with a totally new design. During the '80s, there was only one company that sold superlong extension poles, and that was Tommy Tucker. He actually made a pool that was 80 feet long, but his extension pole was not rigid enough for squeegee work.

Besides, no one had a squeegee that would work that high, except for my new Sörbo 3 × 4 Adjustable Wide-Body squeegee. As a result, I came up with a totally new design. I knew that the extension pole would bend mostly in the middle, so instead of making the traditional Christmas tree design, I developed the first stacked extension pole on the market! It was thin at the top, wide in the middle, and thin at the bottom. Instead of making it from the extruded aluminum that all extension poles were made of, I made it from drone tubing that was very light and very rigid. The 40-foot pole weighed only 12 pounds, full length, which surprised every window cleaner who tried it. I designed my new pole in seven sections, each 6 feet long. The three middle sections were the same dimension, with a 1.5-inch outer diameter (OD). These tubings were micro-fit and flared at one end to make them super-rigid. This was the first stacked extension pole on the market, and if you needed a longer extension pole, you could add 1.5-inch 6-foot sections. Then, the top sections tapered down all the way to the end tip. The very bottom tubing slides inside the number six section, which is designed with a heavy-duty aluminum lock. By reducing one of the 1.5-inch 6-footers in the middle, you made yourself a 30-foot to 36-foot extension pole. If you remove two of the 1.5-inch middle sections, then eliminate the number seven section, and insert section three at the end, where the aluminum lock is in section six, you will have an 18-foot to a 24-foot telescopic pole.

I introduced this new 40-foot Monster pole at the second Southwest window cleaning workshop in Lubbock in 1989. Believe me, there were a lot of surprised window cleaners! Additionally, the ones who already used the Sörbo 3 × 4 Adjustable Wide-Body squeegee were very excited. This was the first time they could clean windows up to the third floor with a squeegee, and they clearly understood why I had developed this Monster pole. Today, this is still the most rigid pole on the market, and it was specially invented for Sörbo 3 × 4 Adjustable Wide-Body squeegees. This is all because you can custom-set the firmness in the rubber.

I also invented the new faster-release handle with the outlet for the safety line on top of the upper jaw so you can attach it to the Monster pole. Just in case the squeegee comes off, it will prevent it from falling down and hurting somebody. The industry has grown tremendously since I invented the Monster pole. Many years later, in the mid-2000s, the carbon fiber water-fed extension poles started to come to the U.S. and became very popular. I didn't know too much about them because I didn't have an interest in water-fed poles. I was strictly manufacturing and inventing for the squeegee market, and I didn't know if they would be rigid enough for squeegee work.

As a result, I stopped production of the Monster poles for a few years. Recently, however, I have had people ask me to start producing them again. When the window cleaners ask for something, I always listen, and I like to be there to help them! In the 1980s, you needed two poles to do the windows that were high up. So, I invented the Twin Ledge Angle, the first ledger with the squeegee and the washer at opposite ends, so you could first wash the window with the Sörbo Yellow Jacket sleeve and then turn it around and squeegee the window. Therefore, you needed only one extension pole after that. Of course, my new Sörbo Cobra Flipper that I had recently designed was greatly appreciated by the professional window cleaning market.

The water-fed pole industry has grown in leaps and bounds since Mr. Tommy Tucker, the king of water-fed poles, first introduced them in 1950. I had the blessing of talking to Tommy at many of the trade shows. It was years ago, but I still remember him as being a very nice man. Window cleaners have asked me for many years why I don't get into the water-fed market. And I always tell them that I don't think it is my place to be there. I'm strictly for the squeegee market, and I will do what I'm good at: introducing original inventions. I'd like to be known as the original in the future! For many years, we have been the only company manufacturing in the U.S. Everybody else went to China; however, Sörbo products continue to stay faithful to the American people. God bless America!! Today, I am the last living of the three original professional window cleaners who became manufacturers. I'd like the younger generation to know who really made this industry what it is today.

Pictures from our time at the 1988 Building Service Contractors Association International (BSCAI) Convention.

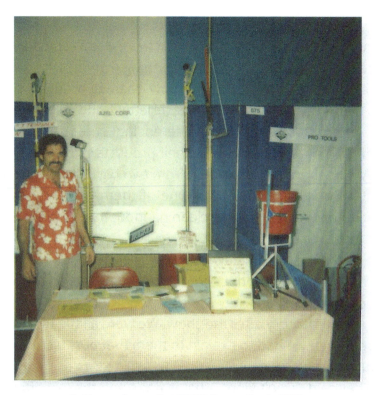
Setting up for my first BSCAI Convention in 1988.

1988: New York City, ISSA Trade Show

We entered our first International Sanitary Supply Association (ISSA) trade show, a great experience for Winnie and me. We were very excited to show our products at the show. While we were setting up, I needed a hammer, and I realized how expensive the trade show was in New York. A hammer cost a hundred dollars! I was totally shocked, to say the least. However, people showed a lot of interest in our new wide-body squeegee, as they had in Houston the year before. But this time, I had Winnie with me. She was busy talking to people, showing products, and taking orders while I was demonstrating all our equipment.

A handful of people asked us if our company was from the Netherlands, and soon, we found out there was a company over there named Sörbo. They sell everything from nail clippers to lumber — everything except window cleaning products. Their logo name is spelled using script-style letters, and our name is in bold letters. But we are in two different industries, so it worked out fine. They're actually selling their products in the U.S. today.

At this show, we got orders from two big distributors who wanted to sell our products. One of them was the biggest distributor for the window cleaning industry in the world at that time, J. Racenstein.

I can't even explain how happy we were, especially to have them take on our product line. The second was a corporate company from Japan. They wanted to come down to California and see our factory after the show. We were a little bit embarrassed when we had to explain to them that our "factory" was in our home!

They said, "Don't worry, that is fine," and the day after the show, three of them came down to Palm Desert to have a meeting in our house. They were our first export distributor! We could barely believe it; we were so excited! They gave us an order for $14,000. We were overwhelmed with joy! We realized at this point that we had a good product. We continued working in our house for a couple of years, and soon, we could afford to rent a small unit in the industrial area in Palm Desert. Well, we worked there for a few years, making our products. It was there that we started to powder-coat the Quicksilver squeegee white. But after a year, the powder coating started to flake off. Consequently, we went back to clear anodizing, and of course, the Black Mamba was still black.

Part IV
Sörbo and the
Beginnings of My Faith

Winnie standing by a very well-cleaned, reflective window.

1988: God Was Speaking to Me

Through the years, I had been drinking together with many buddies, who later on in life passed away because of alcohol-related diseases. Some people actually believed that I would be next on the list. In 1988, my buddy Tommy Södergren and I had been drinking for three days straight, and come Monday morning, when I woke up, sitting on my bed trying to get my mind together, I felt a snapping sound in my heart! I felt like it would jump out of my chest. I got very scared. The first thing that came to my mind was, *Now the time has come for the headstone.* As they'd predicted, I was next on the list.

At that exact time, I heard a voice, loud and clear, saying, "Sören, what is going to happen to your wife and your child if you die?" I looked around, but I was all alone. I had NEVER been to church, except when I went to school in Sweden. We had to go to church and listen to the priest for a week. I had never listened to him enough to learn anything. I was more interested in other things. When I was very young, I remember that Christian people were not very highly talked about in our family because when my mom was a little kid, there was a Pentecostal church on the first floor of their building, and they were screaming in tongues. Mom and my aunt were very scared, they said, so I grew up with a very negative view of Christians.

However, for some reason, I knew that it was God who was speaking to me. I also had a vision. It was like a movie playing in front of me. I could see Winnie and Mindi standing, holding hands and looking at me, and I felt so low. As a result of this shame, tears started to pour out of my eyes, and I was thinking, *How are they going to provide for themselves if I die?* I felt like I had abandoned them. I felt so helpless, and I said, "Oh Lord, if you save my life this time I will never drink again."

Interestingly, my wife had never seen me shed a tear! I did not even know that I could weep. There were many times I wanted to because of my depression, but I could not. And that was the last thing I remember. I don't know if I died or not; only God knows. To my surprise, I woke up in the hospital. I found out later that the ambulance had picked me up. I asked the doctor, "What happened to me? What is wrong with me?"

He said that they didn't find anything wrong with me. I still remember what the voice had said. That afternoon, I walked out of the hospital, and when I was walking across the parking lot, I realized for the first time in many years the craving for alcohol was gone!! I started jumping and laughing with joy! I told my Winnie it must have been God who had talked to me. This was a miracle!! God had set me free from this horrible addiction.

I was so happy that the first thing I did when I got home was to take my crowbar, demolish my big bar, and throw all my booze bottles away. What a day, what a day! This was a good thing because I had just started to market my products, and now I believed I would be able to represent our new company in a better way. This addiction to alcohol had had control over me! Winnie was so happy for me and for this new start in our life. Many times, we had a stressful relationship. My wife had a hard time with me because of my drinking and almost left me three times through the years.

She told her friends, "This is a light at the end of the tunnel." She had had faith that one day, I would quit drinking. Well, on my own, I couldn't. But with God, it was possible! I thank Him every morning! I thank Him for saving my life! I consider myself to be a strong person because I smoked for many years, and I was strong enough to quit that. However, I used snuff, something similar to chewing tobacco, which was very popular in Sweden. It has a high concentration of nicotine. You make a little ball in between your fingers, and push it up underneath your upper lip. That's how you get the nicotine into your bloodstream. It's very potent. I have given it to friends here in America, and they have turned white in the face because they swallowed some of its juice and they were not used to it. That was harder to quit than smoking. However, I quit that too.

Alcohol addiction I was never able to kick until God spoke to me that Monday and answered my request!! Consequently, that is the reason why Mr. Sörbo became a Christian! You may say, *no, you're wrong*. I still was a hardheaded man with a hard heart, but you will find out later in the book what happened.

1988: Sörbo Glide, the First Friction Reducer on the Market, and the New Cleaning Soap

Sörbo Glide friction reducer combined with the Sörbo soap is the first non-suds, professional window cleaning soap on the market. Many people have noticed the benefits of this new combination. Today, I am the only window-cleaning supplies manufacturer with 50 years of experience in window cleaning, and I developed this new cleaning method for a reason. Cleaning windows in the desert is sometimes very difficult in the summertime when the heat rises up to 118 degrees in the shade. One summer, it was 128 degrees. I remember we tried using ice blocks in the bucket to cool down the windows when we cleaned them directly in the sunlight, but it didn't really work that well. Many times, we put more chemicals in the water to make the rubber glide better on the hot window, but the more chemicals you put in your water, the more chemicals you leave on the window, and the glass would actually attract more pollution and more dirt.

In our company, we specialized in high-quality window cleaning, so we got a lot of new customers who were not happy with their previous window cleaner. Many times, when we cleaned the windows for the first time for a new customer, we found a lot of chemicals on the window already, and all you really needed was water because the window already had the chemicals on it. You could see the suds on the glass, and that is probably why the customer didn't like the quality because the windows fogged up very quickly, so I realized I had to develop a new way to be able to get the squeegee to glide without adding the chemical that cleans the window. I came up with the idea to separate the cleaning soap and the glide in the present window cleaning soap, and I talked to a chemist who had the formula for this chemical that I called "the glide." On a hot day, all you have to add to the water is the Sörbo Glide friction reducer. That way, you have the right amount of cleaning powder all the time, and the window stays cleaner longer. It also works as a high-performance friction reducer, so the squeegee rubber will hold up a lot longer. Also, it's very important when you scrape the windows with a Sörbo 6-inch razor blade scraper. If you use the light color strip washer, it rinses the dirt out from the fibers automatically, and the washer stays nice and clean. For a long time, I realized that suds slow you down. The suds increase the amount of water sticking to the window frame and make the detailing rag very wet, so we discovered that you could actually clean the whole outside of the house with only one surgical rag. Before that, we had to have two of them for the outside and two for the inside. The glide also keeps the window wet for longer in the heat. It might be different back East, where you have more humidity, but the result is the same: it will improve because of this new chemical combination, and the benefit is that the windows stay clean longer, and they get really black and shiny when you look at them. The customers pointed that out many times, and they really appreciated it. Some customers asked how the windows could stay clean for so long when we did the cleaning, compared to their previous window cleaners, and I explained to them that the window doesn't have any chemicals on it when we are done. I used to teach this in my seminars, and I heard a few window cleaners say, "I don't want the window to stay clean longer; then I have less work," but I told them high quality is what gives you a lot more customers in the long run because they will tell their friends about your high quality. This is how we got 100 percent of our new customers: through word of mouth.

You can see my videos on YouTube showing how to clean windows without suds.

1989: Deciding to Enter the IWCA Competition

I was serious. I built a complete competition window, and three months before the convention, I started to run a couple of miles every morning. I practiced on the windows every afternoon, looking at the timing. I had broken the world record many times. I was excitedly looking forward to the competition, and I was going to be the only manufacturer who had entered. Well, the race started, my turn came up, and I did all three windows, but, to my surprise, one of the judges — the owner of one of the biggest window cleaning companies in the country — decided to disqualify me on my first run. That really bothered me. I had invested so much time and money, and there I only got to do one pass, and I was disqualified. I have never forgotten that, and I never entered the competition again. I knew it would have been even harder later on due to my rising popularity. The next year, the convention was held in San Diego, and Winnie entered. She took bronze; I was so proud of her.

Winnie for the win!

1989: Moving into Our First Warehouse and the Most Reliable Employee

As you already know, many years earlier, I had sent for Tommy Södergren to come from Sweden and work for me. He was an outstanding employee. During the eight years he was working for me, he was never homesick. You could set the clock by this guy. He always came at the same time every morning — never late. Well, our manufacturing was growing, and Tommy was running the window-cleaning truck with two other guys. Everything was working well, and it was a great source of capital.

One day, all of a sudden, I heard Kay, our office manager, telling me that Tommy had started to have difficulty breathing. We told him to go to the doctor, but he said, "Crap, I don't believe in doctors," and he kept working. Soon, he had to sit down and gasp for air. That's when we took him to the hospital in Palm Springs, and they did a complete checkup. At the hospital, the doctor discovered that not only did he have lung cancer, but his lungs were also half full of water, and his whole body had cancer. He was hooked up to oxygen immediately. The doctor gave him two weeks to live.

I immediately realized I had to sell my window cleaning business because Tommy was key to its success, so I placed an ad in the *Los Angeles Times*. I had some really good customers, including, as mentioned before, Mr. & Mrs. Walt Disney's home every month for 12 years. To my surprise, the first person who called me purchased the company. This took place only one week after God had spoken to me and set me free from alcohol. Tommy was my drinking buddy.

The doctor sent him to Riverside Hospital. When I went to visit, I told him, for the first time, that God had spoken to me and set me free from my addiction. Winnie and I had been talking about this, and she said, "You can tell Tommy 'Pray to God and He will help you,'" and I forwarded that message to Tommy.

The last day when I went to visit him, he said, "Samuelsson, you are crazy — you believing that blip, blip."

Well, it was Winnie who had said it. It was the last time I talked to Tommy. Of course, when he went home to Sweden, he told people that I had become religious, and the rumors spread fast!

Some people asked me, "Is it true what I hear? Are you religious now?" but I wasn't. Even though I had heard God's voice, I did not want to have anything to do with Jesus.

But it was another old drinking buddy who said that he'd had a similar experience to mine. His name was Tim, and he became a born-again Christian and was set free from his addiction. He visited Tommy at the hospital in Falun, Sweden. That's when Tommy told Tim that I had become religious. But at the time, I wasn't.

One day, I was working underneath my '39 LaSalle in the back of my house when I heard a voice outside the gates. "Sören, are you there?" It was Tim, my old drinking buddy, who had come to tell me about Jesus. Even though I had heard God's voice and He had saved my life, I didn't want anything to do with Him. As a matter of fact, I got really upset about having people asking me all the time. Consequently, I refused to talk to Tim. He just upset me more, and I didn't even come out and talk to him, so he left. I hadn't seen him for seven years. Can you imagine? He came all the way from Sweden just to talk to me about Jesus, and I was so rude! Well, time went on, and I did see him nine years later; that's when I asked him for forgiveness.

1989: Introducing the First 48-Inch Single Sörbo 3 × 4 Adjustable Wide-Body Squeegee in the World. (This Was a Single Channel; the Eliminator Came Later)

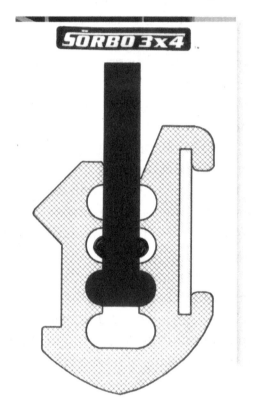

A graphic of our 3 × 4 Adjustable Wide-Body squeegee.

In 1988, I was interviewed by *American Window Cleaner Magazine*, for issue #12. Rod Woodward and Rich Fabry, the founders of the magazine, wrote a four-page article about my products. In the opening statement, Rich said,

Sören Samuelsson, the founder of Sörbo Products, has produced products that are revolutionizing the window cleaning industry. If someone had told me that there was going to be a 48-inch squeegee developed, I would have expected to see it as part of a circus act, not a tool that could actually be used professionally. Likewise, his determination to make it possible to reuse the squeegee rubber — that is, to shave off strips of rubber to create a new sharp edge rather than simply tossing it out — is nothing less than revolutionary. Sören is friendly and personable and on his way to becoming part of the American Dream.

The previous 36-inch Sörbo 3 × 4 Adjustable Wide-Body squeegee was a revolutionary size, and most window cleaners thought this was the limit, but I didn't think so. I realized that the channel was so rigid it needed so little pressure, so I developed the first 48-inch squeegee. This was just a single channel, and at that time, we did not have 48-inch squeegee rubber, so I had to use two 24-inch squeegee rubbers. I invented and designed a special clip that I installed in the middle of the channel, and that clip squeezed both ends together so it didn't leave any streaks. After trying it, we found out it worked great, so I made a 48-inch mold for natural rubber. The same as with the 36-inch squeegee, in the second adjustment, the rubber needed to be one step out from the bottom. That way, it adapts to the uneven window surface perfectly well. We introduced this new 48-inch Sörbo 3 × 4 Adjustable Very Wide squeegee at the second IWCA convention in Florida in 1990. I invented the revolutionary Eliminator in 1997.

1990: Sörbo Stops Making the White Squeegee Rubber

In 1986, I invented the white T-shaped squeegee rubber in order to get more adjustments in the 3 × 4 adjustable squeegee, but it is also the only universal squeegee rubber on the market. I designed it so it fits both the brass and the stainless steel squeegees. This was the first white, non-marking, high-quality squeegee rubber in the world. Window cleaners said it held up a lot longer than the traditional rubber, and that is because we used less filler in the compound. Carbon is a filler that makes the rubber black, but it also makes the squeezy rubber less durable, so it will wear the rubber out faster. But we had a problem: they left black marks on the wallpaper around the bathroom mirrors, especially where they had the wallpaper up against the mirror.

In the '90s, we started to add a little bit of the carbon to our compound to make it glide better on the window, but we didn't want to add too much, which would reduce the rubber's lifespan. So that the Sörbo Glide would reduce the friction and also prolong the rubber's lifespan, we wanted to produce the longest-lasting rubber on the market. But it is also very important to have a very high-quality compound, especially when we had the technology to trim the squeegee rubber with the Docket. If you buy squeegee rubber of bad quality, it will leave streaks on the window from the first use. I have seen videos on YouTube where window cleaners claim that they have to break in the squeegee rubber before it works because it leaves streaks, but I have explained to some window cleaners that a squeegee rubber should work 100 percent right out of the box.

This new term, "breaking in," does not make sense. If you have a high-quality compound, a good way to make a perfect edge, and also very high quality control, then it should work right away. In our factory, every squeegee rubber is passed through sensitive fingers and periodically inspected with microscopes. The process that produces sharp corners on the squeegee rubber is very high-tech. It is very difficult to achieve if you don't know how to do it, and it will leave fine streaks when you squeegee the window.

That's why they have to break it in before it works. You practically have to wear the rubber out until you pass down below the defective surface. That is far from high quality. To avoid streaks, the corner of the rubber has to be totally sharp. You can buy a Sörbo Docket squeegee blade sharpener and sharpen those new rubbers, LOL.

Winnie (right) and our daughter Mindi (left) at a convention in 1992.

Working on my '39 Caddy in 1990.

Pulling the '39 Caddy together.

The '39 Caddy, custom built, still in progress.

1993: Moving into a Bigger Place

Now, the business was really taking off, and we needed a bigger place. I remember my mom and dad visited from Sweden, and my aunt came from Catskill, New York, to visit, and they were helping us to assemble squeegees. This was when we introduced the white, wide-body, powder-coated squeegees for the first time. They looked really cool with their blue label. But a year later, the powder coating started to flake because the aluminum started to oxidize underneath, where it was constantly in contact with chemicals. So, we went back to using the clear anodizing again. However, we still made the original Black Mamba. We continued to go to the ISSA, BSCAI, and IWCA window cleaning trade shows and conventions every year.

I used to donate reproductions of my paintings at the auction every year, and they sold for up to $750 each. I still have dozens of paintings left. And they will be up for sale through this special website, creativeartbysorbo.com.

As the reader knows, another hobby I had was working on old cars from the '30s to the '50s. Through the years, I have had dozens of cars that I purchased through ads, and at the Pomona Swap Meet and Classic Car Show. They were very easy to sell in Sweden when I came here to California. I fixed them up and kept them for a while. Later on, I shipped them to Sweden, and I made a couple of thousand dollars from each car. One day, a friend of mine named Bob, who owned a gas station in Indio, asked if I would be interested in a 1960 Cadillac Biarritz convertible. One of his customers wanted to sell it. So, I went and looked at it, and when I met the owner, I discovered that his name was Mr. Asher! He was a friend of Prince Bertil of Sweden. Mr. Asher told me he and Prince Bertil had become friends in the 1940s when they joined the High Society Club in London, and that Asher's wife was a well-known opera singer. He was so excited to talk about the old days with me because I was Swedish!

Anyway, the car needed a new top, but it was very straight, had no dents, and he was the only owner. I purchased the car for $500. Today, those cars are worth over $100,000. I kept that car for ten years, and then I sold it to a guy in Sweden. It has been in a few car magazines. When I had it, it was a golden green, the original color. I remember I got $15,000 for the car when I sold it. This was in the beginning when prices started to increase for classic cars in Scandinavia. It had a big block, 390 hp V8 engine, with three two-barrel carburetors. It was extremely fast for such a big car.

But one day, I got tired of that hobby. I kept six of the cars: a 1959 Chevy Impala two-door coupe, a 1971 Cadillac DE convertible, a 1941 Plymouth Coupe, and three 1939 Cadillac LaSalles, two of which were two-door coupes. I've always liked original cars, but in 1990, I saw one made into a street rod. I had never seen anybody do that before, so I decided to build my own street rod. In 1991, I started to take the whole car apart, and I welded the chassis. Later on, I reshaped the entire body. I did everything that needed to be done to make the car Sörbo-imagined. I did all the welding necessary to change the front end, and then I built a 454 V8. I even put a 700-R4 transmission in it. I also built a 9-inch Ford rear axle with 9-11 gear ratio. I shortened and tubed it and put 19-inch Mickey Thompson tires on the back. I also altered the roof by 3.5 inches, picked up an electric sunroof from a Saab at the junkyard, and installed that, too. I wanted to get a look that resembled me, and soon, I was ready to introduce a very unique street rod made by Sörbo. Funny thing is, I am still working on that car 26 years later. I have modified it step-by-step to be "me," as they say. I have not even had a chance to put a final paint job on it, but it is one of a kind.

Through the years, I built bigger and bigger engines. Right now, I am building my third engine, and this is the biggest one I have built so far. It's a 632 Brodix aluminum block with a 1050 Dominator, a 500-hp two-stage nitrous fogger sprayer, and all the goodies for a fast quarter-mile run at the drag strip.

I have been very fortunate to learn many different trades throughout my life. This is because I've never been afraid to ask people how to do things. I asked technical questions and then just went ahead and did it! That's the way I learned. Some people are too proud to ask. I have met many people who act like they know everything and never give themselves a chance to learn a thing. If you remember, I went to welding school and auto mechanics school, where I learned a lot. I was taught how to rebuild engines and how to draw blueprints. Those skills came in handy when I started to invent new window-cleaning equipment. I always tell young people to travel the world and to learn different trades. Too many young people today think they are going to start at the top, and this is why they never get a chance to learn anything. I tell them, "You have to start from the bottom and work yourself up to where you learn more and more and earn more."

I had a job where I didn't make very much money at all, but I learned new trades, which I benefited from in my manufacturing business. In the '70s, I learned how to build homes when I worked part-time in construction. I developed the skills to remodel my own house, which was almost the same way I learned how to remodel my own cars: in steps over the years. All that I learned in my life I learned from hands-on practice. I even worked at the gas station for a few months because I didn't have work. I didn't make very much money doing that, but I never stayed home because I couldn't make the money I needed if I had no job. That's the problem with many young people today: they don't develop new skills because they refuse to work when the pay isn't high enough. All the while, they miss out on the opportunity to learn something new.

1993: Invention #6. Twin Ledge Angle. Patented, October 26, 1993

In 1993, I created one more product that was developed because of the 40-foot Monster pole.

You can see here again the chain reaction from the previous invention. I realized that sometimes, when you clean windows with a deep ledge, it is difficult to get to the bottom of the window. And, because of the 40-foot pole, it was even more difficult because now we were getting up to heights to clean windows with a squeegee that we had never reached before. The higher up you clean, the harder it is to finish off the bottom section of the window. The Twin Ledge Angle was a totally new ledger tool that I invented because of the Monster pole, and with this new device, you can adjust the angle. This was only possible because of my Sörbo 3 × 4 Adjustable Wide-Body squeegee, which allows you to adjust the squeegee rubber out one step into the second setting. By doing that, for the first time, you could get all the way down to the bottom of the window. I also designed it so you have a T-bar with the washer at the opposite end. You really have to look at my video to fully understand how it works. The advantage is that your starting point will be closer against the building in order to finish the window. With this device, you always start to wash the window with the washer on the top. Then, you proceed to wash the majority of the window panel, and when you get to the bottom of the window, you tilt the twin angle over. Now, the washer is automatically at the bottom, so you can finish off the bottom of the window all the way down to the frame. Now, the squeegee automatically ends up in the upper elevation. To start squeegeeing, turn the Twin Ledge Angle a half-turn around so that the squeegee faces the window. If you have the right angle adjusted when starting against the building and walking backward, you should finish the window all the way down. You can also clean atrium windows from the top using the push method or stand below and use the pull method. Because of this ledger, you need only one Monster pole. Before I invented the Twin Ledge Angle, you actually needed two poles: one to wash the window and the second one for the squeegee.

A year later, a window cleaner friend of mine, Jerry Rigdon, invented the ledger. That also worked exceptionally well because of the technology in the Sörbo 3 × 4 Adjustable Wide-Body squeegee. Also, Mr. LongArm introduced an extension pole that was bent in the same fashion, with an end tip that swiveled. The inventor demonstrated this at the trade shows. He was, as a matter of fact, the first one on the market who demonstrated how to fan the window with an extension pole. I remember that he was scared to death to fly, so he would drive his car to all the trade shows.

1994: Sörbo Made More Instruction Videos

I knew that in order to teach people how to use the new equipment I invented, I needed to teach the new window cleaning techniques I had developed. I had already offered seminars for years, which were a great success with our distributors. Anywhere between 20 and 40 people attended. However, my goal was to reach the people whom I didn't have the opportunity to meet, so I came up with the idea of making three different videos. These videos helped people reduce labor and increase their production. The three videos I produced were called *Window Cleaning: The Z Method*, the L method video, and the upside-down U method video. Shortly thereafter, I introduced the reverse stroke method and the 5-degree angle method, which, by turning the squeegee upside down in the handle, is perfect for working with glass ceilings (this is the only squeegee handle of its kind in the world).

VHS copies of *Window Cleaning: The Z Method*,
the first window cleaning instructional videos.

A very important aspect of my new inventions was to introduce a new, simple way of cleaning windows with straight strokes, which reduced the fatigue on one's arm, wrists, and shoulders. Over the years, I have had many window cleaners express their gratitude for my inventions. They told me that they had pain in different joints and muscles for years, but their pain disappeared when they started to use the 36-inch Sörbo 3 × 4 Adjustable Wide-Body squeegee, along with my new window cleaning techniques. Those remarks have brought me great satisfaction.

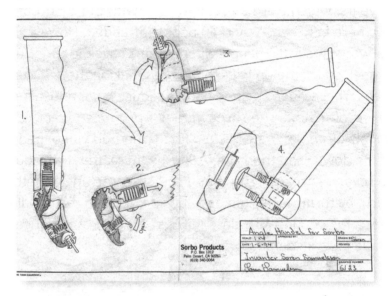

Another invention, without patent, in 1994: the Angle Handle.
The first two-way swivel handle.

1994: Ledgomatic Made for Frames up to 12 Inches Deep: Invention #5: Patent Number 5.175.902

The Ledgomatic was created in the same family of Sörbo squeegees as the Twin Ledge Angle. This invention was a by-product of the 40-foot Monster pole and the Sörbo 3 × 4 Adjustable Wide-Body squeegee. I received a request from Houston Intercontinental Airport asking me to come and look at some windows they were having problems cleaning. They said that they recognized the many innovative products I had developed, so they asked me to look at these windows to see if I could come up with a solution to their problem. They explained that the windows had very deep frames, which made them hard to get to. When I arrived at the airport, I realized that the window frames were 6 inches deep, and the window wall was leaning about 6 degrees outward. Even more challenging was the fact that the windows were 24 feet high. At that time, there was no window cleaning tool in the world that could be used to clean those windows with an extension pole. However, I realized that we had a very rigid Monster pole that I thought might be the perfect solution for this problem. So, I told the supervisor from the cleaning crew that I would try to invent a tool for them. I knew it had to be a semiautomatic device. On the flight back to California, I came up with the idea to make a ledger tool with a rotating squeegee, which, when it reached the bottom of the window frame, would automatically turn forward and finish off the window. And that is how the Ledgomatic was born! Take note; this was also a chain reaction from the Sörbo 3 × 4 Adjustable Wide-Body squeegee, because of the technology in the adjustments that allowed it to move the rubber out in the channel, and also because of the soft rubber that I developed.

Soon after that, I did a seminar at the San Diego International Airport. I was using the prototype at that time, and the guy who cleaned windows there got so excited he actually convinced me to sell him my prototype. He thought it was the greatest thing since sliced bread! One can actually adjust the depth of this device to clean windows which have from 6 to 12-inch-deep window seals.

The Ledgomatic earned me an innovation award at the ISSA Interclean show in Amsterdam on May 8, 2000. This is the biggest commercial cleaning show in the world. There, I was recognized for my deep-frame window cleaning tool. I even received a special plaque from the United States Patent Office!

1994: Introducing the S-Channel, Also Named the Quicksilver Channel

I came up with a great improvement — a totally new design — on the Sörbo 3 × 4 Adjustable Wide-Body squeegee that I had invented ten years earlier. This would make the squeegee clean closer to the window corners. I started to cut it on a 40-degree angle at each end, and this became the most popular design next to the Cobra channel. To make this squeegee, I had to invent new equipment to cut the 40-degree angle. By designing and building this new machine, I reduced the manufacturing time by 75 percent. As I explained before, when you invent new equipment, you also have to invent new tools to manufacture it. Through the years, we have featured a special Sörbo edition of this squeegee once a year at the IWCA convention. We used to give out 200 squeegee channels at that show. Every time they opened the doors for the convention, the window cleaners would flock straight to our booth to pick up their new custom color of the year. It has been such a joy to meet so many of you guys.

1994: Inventing the First Wide-Body Squeegee with Plastic End Plugs to Prevent Scratching Windows, and the Cobra Squeegee Was Born. Patented, January 17, 1995

Ten years earlier, Sörbo had revolutionized the world with our Black Mamba 3 × 4 Adjustable Wide-Body squeegee, and now almost ten years later, we again proved to the window cleaning world that we are the greatest inventors in window cleaning history. I came up with one more revolutionary invention: the first squeegee with plastic end plugs with a 40-degree angle at each end to reach into the corners better. I am the only professional window cleaner in the world who has a squeegee with two patents.

My new idea came to me because a window cleaner I knew was using a 26-inch Sörbo 3 × 4 Wide-Body squeegee. He would do two vertical strokes to clean the windows, but sometimes, he would hit the window when reaching up to complete the second stroke. When he did this, I could hear the squeegee hitting the window. That didn't sound good, so I told him he had to be careful. This prompted me to start thinking that if he was a professional window cleaner having this challenge, then there might be more people with the same problem. That's when I got the idea to design the first safety-end plugged squeegee in the world! I called it the Cobra channel! I also made it clipless so you wouldn't have to worry about end clips. I knew window cleaners often lost the end clips on their squeegees at the workplace, and they couldn't continue working because they hadn't brought spare end clips. If that happened to a high-rise window cleaner, he would have to rappel all the way down to the street to attach new end clips. I made one end plug with friction points so that when you insert the squeegee blade, you have to do it from the end where the website address is shown on the channel label, and then force it through the second plug where the Sörbo logo is situated. However, some window cleaners prefer two-end clips, so we started to insert an extra end clip on the opposite end.

I also teach people how they can benefit from the plastic end plugs when they do pole work. The plastic end plugs will not scratch the frame because the plugs are made of a special plastic compound that is very soft and slippery. The way to take advantage of this feature is to cut the end of the rubber a quarter-inch shorter. Now, the rubber will be recessed in the channel. The channel is longer than the squeegee rubber, which leaves room for the vinyl seal around the edge of the window frame. The result is that the rubber doesn't bend when you slide the squeegee end plug against the window frame. However, you cannot keep the metal end clip in this channel because the clip will scratch the frame. As I said earlier, it does not need end clips, and because of this technology, you have less detailing. Also, if you drop the squeegee with the plastic end plugs, you have less of a chance of damaging the aluminum channel ends. Another benefit is that if the plug breaks, you can purchase replacement plugs along with the installation tool that I invented.

The same was true of the new end plug: I had to invent new machines to manufacture this new squeegee. The most time-consuming challenge of this product was to assemble the plug without scratching the plastic off, so I invented and made a totally new debarring machine that could do the job.

Talking about the Cobra, I just remember something that happened many years later, after I became a Christian. Remember, I always had a short temper. Growing up, that got me into a lot of trouble. But, once I became a born-again Christian, God took that away from me. For example, one year, we went to the Amsterdam cleaning show in the Netherlands. As soon as we finished setting up our booth, my tradition was to walk around and visit with the other manufacturers, most of whom I knew pretty well. I walked over to a booth to greet them, and to my surprise, I found what looked like my Cobra squeegee channel in their display. It looked exactly like our product, but the end plug was a little bit of a different color. I said to my friend, "It looks like you copied my Cobra channel."

He said, "Well, it's not exactly the same as yours." He tried to explain why it wasn't like my squeegee. So I asked for a sample. I told him I would take it to my patent attorney in Long

Beach, California, to see what he thought. I thanked him for the sample, and then I went back to my booth. When I came back to my booth, I talked to my employees, who are also Christians, and explained what had happened.

I said, "I leave it in God's hands. I wonder what will happen to them?"

My wife said, "Don't talk like that!"

"Well, maybe I shouldn't. I can't deny that I was thinking that way, but I won't mention it again," I said.

When I returned to California, my attorney agreed that it was an exact copy of my squeegee, and because I still had a patent, he sent them a letter and told them they had to stop making that squeegee or we would take legal action against them. They agreed to stop the project. The next year, the ISSA trade show was in Las Vegas, and my attorney told me to go over to their booth to see if they were still displaying that squeegee. After setting up our booth, I went over to their booth just before the opening of the show to see my friend. But when I got there, to my surprise, their booth was empty! I talked to their sales rep, and he said that the whole shipment had gotten lost and that he had had to call all their distributors in the U.S. and ask them to send them some equipment for the show. When I saw this, I realized again you don't mess with God's children. If you do, there are going to be consequences.

I have to tell you a similar story, but it wasn't the same because my patent had already expired on my Sörbo 3 × 4 Black Mamba Adjustable Wide-Body squeegee. This involved another manufacturer whom I knew pretty well from the trade shows. At the Atlanta trade show, this particularly nice man came and told me, "Sörbo, I got something I have to tell you!"

"Okay. What is it, mister?" I exclaimed.

To my surprise, he said, "I have copied your squeegee!"

Although this man had done the same thing, this time, because I was a changed man, I said, "No kidding! I am impressed! Thank you, mister!" and shook his hand. He looked at me like he hadn't expected that answer, but later on, when I saw the squeegee, I realized he'd respected my design by changing it. It was not an exact copy of my design, but it was the wide-body squeegee, after all. Well, I knew then that my Sörbo 3 × 4 Adjustable Wide-Body squeegee had changed the window cleaning world. This was just the beginning. It's amazing how comforting it is to have a friend like Jesus. Later on, when more and more window cleaning manufacturers started to duplicate my 3 × 4 wide-body squeegee, I had a few faithful window cleaners calling me every time somebody made a copy of my products. They asked me if I wasn't upset. I told them, "If you look at it the positive way, this will help more window cleaners to try to get used to a wide-body squeegee."

The only time I get upset is when some people think they're going to make a lot of money by making their own squeegee, and they make an exact copy of my invention. But then I remember God is looking out for me. God decides, of course, what happens to them. I leave the consequences to God. He deals with these circumstances as He knows best. He works in mysterious ways.

Through the years, I have acknowledged a few copycats coming into this industry. It is usually a person who doesn't have any sense of respect for the original inventor, but as you can see from the previous copycats, I had someone take care of that. They are usually smaller companies that are trying to break into the industry. They come, and they go. They spend a lot of money for a while, but usually, our faithful window cleaners will stay with the original instead of using an imitation. After a few years, they realize that they are not making any money, and they stop making the products. I was at a trade show in Singapore, and I walked past a booth that looked exactly like that of one of the biggest manufacturers in the window cleaning industry at that time. This person had copied every product to a T. He was around for a few years, and then he ran out of money and disappeared. That's the way it goes when you're a copycat; if you don't have the knowledge and the technical mind to invent something yourself, then you shouldn't be in this industry at all. Invest the money in something that you can feel proud of.

Most window cleaning companies have changed their wide-body squeegees to fit their own special niche. You can see what company these niche products belong to. Like the automobiles in the 1950s, you knew if a car was a Chevy, Mopar, Buick, or Ford. I respect them for that. Today, a window cleaner can tell, just by looking at the squeegee, who the manufacturer is. I have developed over a dozen products through the years, and you can see my inventions mirrored in most of the products in the window cleaning industry. I have been very blessed to see that my inventions are leading this industry. Most window cleaners are writing about them in *American Window Cleaner Magazine*. They are now acknowledging how much my inventions have changed the industry since I started to invent new products 48 years ago when we had only one kind of squeegee.

1994: A Very Good Year

I developed more products that year than I ever had in the past.

Although the 36-inch Sörbo 3 × 4 Adjustable Wide-Body squeegee started to be very popular, I had a few window cleaners complain that the squeegee rubber left a streak right in front of the handle.

We replaced the squeegee rubbers immediately, thinking there was something wrong with the rubber from our factory.

We have the highest quality control rules in our industry. Every squeegee rubber is hand-checked by very sensitive fingers and inspected periodically under a microscope. All the rubber we sent out had passed the quality control tests, but we continued to get more complaints. I asked the window cleaners to send me samples of their defective items so we could inspect the rubber. We discovered the damage was only on the 36-inch rubber, and the defect was right in the center on all of them.

By this time, a lot more window cleaners started to use our 36-inch wide-body squeegee. Most of them had been using the 18-inch squeegees because that was the standard size squeegee used to perform the fanning cleaning method. When using the fanning method, window cleaners always put the handle horizontally in the holster. Can you imagine putting the handle with a 36-inch squeegee attached horizontally in a holster and walking into a house? You would have the door frames hanging all over you! The holsters purchased in those days were made of leather. The new 36-inch Sörbo 3 × 4 Adjustable Wide-Body squeegee became so popular that window cleaners would slide it down vertically into the holster normally used for their 18-inch squeegee, which was inserted horizontally. And because of that, the leather holster was too abrasive, and it made an imprint right in front of the rubber, right in front of the handle grip. I realized it was time to invent a new squeegee-friendly type of holster.

Smiling with all eight of my patents, mid-'90s.

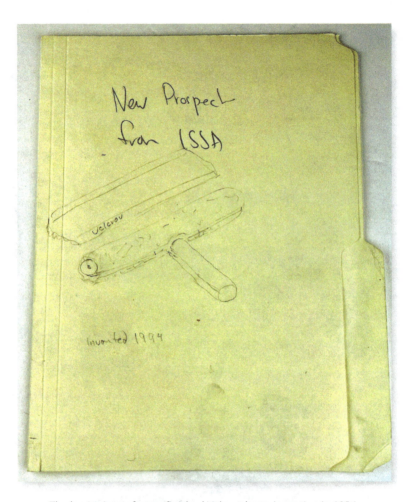

The beginnings of an unfinished Velcro sleeve invention in 1994.

1994: Developing the First Nylon Holster in the World

Sörbo Products introduced this new holster in three different colors: gray, purple, and black. That was the beginning of a more colorful industry. Our newest product was a dual holster for two squeegees. Now, a window cleaner could carry an 18-inch and a 36-inch squeegee at the same time. We never had another squeegee rubber leaving streaks after that.

I also developed a little pouch in the same colors for carrying steel wool. At the time, all the belts on the market were too soft and flimsy. Eventually, they curled up inside the holsters and were more like a tube instead of a flat belt. Window cleaners walked around with their tools hanging down too low. This inspired me to develop the most rigid squeegee belt on the market. I included an extra loop so window cleaners could carry our new 6-inch scraper and my new 5-inch detailing squeegee. These inventions were another first in the window cleaning industry. After that, two other major window cleaning manufacturers followed our lead and made their own nylon holsters. It was clear for all to see that the industry was evolving step-by-step because of my inventions.

1994. Inventing the First Custom Swivel Handle That Pivots in Two Directions.

The first two-way swivel handle that I invented in 1994, with the first Wide-Body, 3 x 4 adjustable squeegee prototype, made from hard wood.

This would be the first squeegee handle that could pivot sideways and up and down. It could be adjusted to five different angles ranging from zero to 90 degrees in both directions. For this new handle, I envisioned a totally new automatic fast-release mechanism. Our pivoting handle would be the result of a lot of new technology, which we would imagine, create, and implement in our new invention. I was certain this was going to be another game changer in the window cleaning industry. However, Winnie was getting tired of not having enough money for food. We were a family business, so we did not have any private investors. In the middle of my patent application, she said, "If you don't stop spending money on patents, I'm going to divorce you!"

Of course, she was just kidding — I hoped. Her comment was really a way of pleading with me not to spend more money than we could afford. I knew that she was serious about that, so in the middle of the patent application, I called my patent attorney in Long Beach and told him what my "boss" had said, and I stopped the project for this new revolutionary handle.

Sometimes, I had my doubts that the new handle would be a very big seller because of the amount of new technology we had put into its design and because of the number of parts required to build it. I believe it was a message from the Man Upstairs, and I listened to my Winnie. Since we are the only window cleaning equipment manufacturer that has all of its products made in the U.S., the new handle would have been quite expensive. I realize now that anybody would be able to see this invention and copy it right away. I know that most big companies wouldn't even bother to buy this "toy." It would mostly be the one-man companies that liked a lot of "toys." I said to my wife, "You might be right."

Although the idea for a pivoting handle was mine, over the years, we have seen most companies eventually come up with ideas similar to my invention. I think that's good, but it is really funny that I invented this revolutionary handle, but we are the only window cleaning equipment manufacturer that does not make even one. That's okay, though, because it is still good to see that my idea sprang to life anyway.

1994: The 6-Inch Flexible Sörbo Scraper, with Swivel Handle

Through the years, window cleaners have learned that when Sörbo Products comes out with a new item, it is made in the U.S. For some time, I had realized that the window scrapers most companies produced were not very good. They were too stiff, and from time to time, they would scratch the glass. I have worked with every window scraper on the market, and they did not apply even pressure across the width of the scraper's blade. This resulted in too much pressure in certain places on the blade and not enough pressure on others. In certain places, the blade didn't even scrape the glass, and you actually had to go back and forth many times before you could remove the paint or other sticky particles from the glass. Often, poorly designed window scrapers were not effective because not all glass is made with a smooth, flat surface. This could be a disaster if you didn't use our Sörbo Glide friction reducer in your window cleaning solution. But even then, I wanted to design a scraper that would be 100 percent effective. I borrowed an idea from the technology in my Sörbo 3 × 4 Adjustable Wide-Body squeegee where you can move the squeegee rubber out, step-by-step, to make the rubber more flexible so that it adapts to the uneven window surface, and I applied it to the new scraper.

Through the years, I have demonstrated this super scraper in my seminars. You can also see it in my videos (on YouTube?), where I teach the window cleaners that I can fan a window like you do with a squeegee and remove all the water immediately. If you went to the Las Vegas IWCA convention in 2023, I was demonstrating this phenomenal scraper, and I offered people $100 if they could show me that their different brand name scraper could fan the window like I did. I never had to pay $100, but I have challenged window cleaners like this for many, many years.

It is really funny because one of my friends who does a popular podcast on YouTube calls this "the widow-maker." This is a scraper for people who have already had experience with other scrapers. But you still have to be very careful when you start using this scraper. It is extremely sharp because we use carbon steel in our razor blades, and you can't find a sharper blade anywhere else. The only setback is, when you use the scraper, you have to remove the blade in the evening and dry it, otherwise, it will rust overnight, and that will surely scratch your windows the next time you use it. But it is sharper than stainless steel blades and really cuts and removes everything from the window in one pass.

Something to remember when you scrape particles off glass: Don't attack it by pushing straight on. Instead, use the same motion as when you cut a tomato. Cut it off with the sliding motion instead of pushing it off, and you will see it works so much easier. Also, remember not to hold the scraper like a jackhammer. Instead, hold it like a pencil. Watch my video on YouTube for better understanding because this scraper does not need very much pressure at all.

Besides the new scraper, I also invented the first Sörbo Products nylon scraper holster for 6-inch scrapers. It is designed with a brass insert inside the holster to keep it from cutting through the nylon webbing. This scraper holster works for most of the scrapers on the market.

1994. Introducing the First Silicone Squeegee Rubber in the World

Because of our Eliminator 3 × 4 Adjustable Wide-Body squeegee, I didn't know the size limit of this revolutionary wide-body squeegee, and I wanted to make them as long as possible. When I looked at all the big storefronts downtown in all the big cities where they have windows that are extremely wide and reach all the way up to the ceiling, it didn't make sense to me that window cleaners were struggling to work with an 18-inch squeegee. I said to myself, *There's got to be a better and easier way for these poor guys to clean those windows.*

Before I invented the Eliminator, we never had a squeegee rubber over 36 inches long. In fact, I had made a mold for and had started to manufacture a 48-inch natural synthetic squeegee rubber, but it was short-lived because we could not keep a constant thickness across the whole length of the rubber. So, I started to extrude the natural synthetic rubber, but that did not work because it changed the structure of our famous compound that I had developed. But then I got the idea to introduce a new silicone blade! Incredibly, by formulating the right compound, I found it worked extremely well. That's when Sörbo Products introduced the first silicone squeegee rubber in the world, which turned out to be a winner! Sörbo shocked the window cleaning world not only with silicone rubber but also with the longest squeegee rubber ever made. We produced it in 50-foot rolls.

Now, window cleaners could cut squeegee rubber blades at exactly the length they needed, without any waste. But here you see, again, the reason I was the first one to come out with a good silicone squeegee blade was because of the previous invention: the Sörbo 3 × 4 Eliminator.

A few years later, a different rubber company tried to duplicate my silicone rubber, but the quality was not very good, so they soon stopped marketing their poorly made rubber. But isn't that the way life seems to be? A professional window cleaner comes up with the original invention that works best, and then you have new companies with deep pockets buying into the industry. Most of the time, the products don't work as well because the companies do it for the money. Today, much of the competition makes molded silicone blades in shorter lengths, but we are still the only one that markets the longest squeegee rubber in the world, and I know a lot of cleaners who purchased the Docket and used the silicone. The cost is a few cents after trimming it 12 times. And it is so easy to trim; it's like cutting butter.

1994. Developing The Yellow Jacket Washer Sleeve

My first year sewing Yellow Jacket washer sleeves.

In the '90s, microfiber washer sleeves were coming over here from China, and it was something new that people wanted to try. I tried many of them, but I did not feel they were any better than our sleeve. The Yellow Jacket holds a larger amount of water without dripping, and it is made from a very durable material, which has very good scrubbing power. The reason I call it "The Yellow Jacket" is because of its yellow material and black trim remind me of a yellow jacket (the flying insect). One of the great benefits of the Yellow Jacket washer sleeve is that it doesn't spew out a bad aroma when you leave it wet in the bucket. In the 1970s, when I started to clean windows, all the sleeves were made with stainless steel snaps, and brass snaps too close to the sleeve. They were of high quality, but I suppose because of the cost factor, everybody went over to Velcro locking strips. However, the old-timers did not like Velcro. They liked the high-quality brass snaps. I also like quality, so I stuck with it. But we do have one model with Velcro because it closes the sleeve completely up to the handle to prevent the water from collecting inside of the sleeve when you dip it into the bucket.

The Yellow Jacket was especially helpful for those who did route work (route work is a window cleaning term for monthly accounts of storefronts) with an extension pole. Sörbo started something new by inserting abrasive material at each end of the washer sleeve. Window cleaners had an ongoing problem with washer sleeves wearing out at each end of the T-bar too quickly. Therefore, we concentrated on making all the products of high-quality material and craftsmanship so our products and equipment would hold up longer. Our quality can be seen in our squeegee rubber and in the Docket squeegee blade sharpener. Sörbo Products is still the only window cleaning equipment manufacturer in the world that makes a rubber blade sharpener. I've heard people say, "Why do you want window cleaners sharpening your squeegee blades? You will sell fewer squeegee rubbers."

My answer to their question is, "My greatest hope is to save money for the window cleaners, and besides, I'm not that crazy about money. If I have enough just to have a good living, that's all I need."

1994: Inventing a Soft Bucket on the Belt

For a short time, I played around with the idea of making a softer bucket on the equipment belt. I was trying to find an easier way to carry the window washer. I made and tried different designs but finally retired that idea. However, you can see the photo of me in 1994, standing there cleaning with the new softer design. There is always room for designing and developing new products, but because I invented the Quadropod — the high bucket stands — I chose to concentrate on perfecting that design instead. I don't believe in carrying a lot of equipment when I clean windows; I'd rather have a working station where I can hang my equipment. When I was still cleaning windows, many of my customers told me they were impressed with all the equipment I was using. These were products I had invented, which eventually ended up being used throughout the world by industrial and commercial window cleaners.

1994: The First 78-Inch Eliminator on the Market

Our Eliminator squeegee; the world's biggest!

A year before I developed the Eliminator, I developed the first plastic end plug squeegee. I had to design a new channel for the new Cobra squeegee, and because this new channel was more rigid than the Quicksilver channel, we used it for the 48-inch squeegees in the '90s. This new channel was perfect for the Eliminator. And now, with this new design, especially for the squeegee with end plugs, I was able to make even larger squeegees. So, my goal was to make the first 6-foot squeegee in the world, and it would be possible with this new Cobra design. But I also knew that I was going to come up with a totally new framework combination if I was going to be able to develop new, revolutionary squeegees up to 78 inches (or 195 cm) in length. I knew, in sizes like that, you cannot attach the squeegee handle in the center of a 78-inch squeegee and get equal pressure across the whole length. Therefore, I designed this squeegee with an establishing bar that attaches to the main squeegee with two clamps. By doing that, you transfer the pressure points away from the center of the main squeegee that is doing the cleaning job on the window. So, in this case, with a 6.5-foot squeegee, you practically have two 39-inch (97.5 cm) ones. And we already know that they work perfectly well on a window. So, I invented this establishing bar that is roughly 3.5 feet long. And that means that you will have each of those two clamps applying pressure right in the middle of these two 39-inch squeegees. Of course, it's not two separate squeegees, but if you have a little imagination, you'll understand what I mean. So, therefore, a 78-inch (195 cm) Eliminator squeegee works as well as two 39-inch squeegees because they each have a pressure point in the center.

And when you use the Eliminators, you have to have the squeegee rubber on the second setting — one step out from the bottom setting — and the handle will be a few degrees further out from the window, so you have to adjust your handle to where the rubber cleans the window with the corner. If you have the handle too close to the window, the squeegee rubber will go flat on the side and leave water. The Sörbo 3 × 4 Adjustable Eliminator squeegees work excellently by hand and when using an extension pole. And we are strictly using our high-quality silicone squeegee blades, which will save you a lot of money because you cut only the sizes you need from the 50-foot roll. The squeegees are also available in six sizes, from 48 inches (120 cm) to 78 inches (195 cm). But this squeegee will make a window cleaner over $100 an hour. You actually move the same amount of water as five window cleaners every time you move it, and what does that tell you?

1995: Inventing the Sörbo Multi-Squeegee

Sörbo showing off the benefits of the first multi-squeegee model.

One of my seminars for distributors, teaching
window cleaning in Portland, Oregon.

Through the years, we had a lot of clients who needed their
French windows cleaned. Cleaning French windows is a pain
in the frame, as we say. It is very time-consuming work with
a small squeegee. Some homes had dozens of those little
square windows. This gave me the idea to create a squeegee
that had between two and six little squeegees side-by-side
with an adjustable opening in between them for the frame. By
using such a multibladed squeegee, in a single stroke, a window
cleaner could reduce the labor it takes to remove the water from
the window. That's when the Sörbo Multi-Squeegee was born!
Most people in the window cleaning industry know that Sörbo
is still the only company that makes custom sizes of squeegees
for window cleaners. We can cut any custom-sized squeegee for
our customers' windows, so you can clean most windows in one
stroke. The Sörbo Multi-Squeegee was the result of creating the
Eliminator squeegee line with the extra support clamps on the
channel that would separate the pressure points on the larger
squeegee channels for even pressure. As with most of my other

inventions, the Multi-Squeegee was developed as a result of my previous invention, very much like a chain reaction. If you look for my YouTube videos, you can watch and learn how to clean French windows and other multipaned windows with the Sörbo Multi-Squeegee. If you are a commercial window cleaner and you have monthly accounts, I recommend you purchase at least one Multi-Squeegee. When I had the window cleaning company, we would custom-cut squeegees for most of our customers. We had shelves in our van with names for those special accounts, which allowed us to clean most of our clients' windows in one stroke. It is difficult to clean a window faster than that. You can watch Sörbo demonstrate how to close off the last pass on the window without leaving water and how to start every cleaning pass without leaving water. Very helpful for beginners. Also, there are many effective and time-saving techniques.

In 1995, I added one more patent to the high bucket stand. My new design was made with plastic. In that design, I made a hole in the bucket where I added the tubing that I used for my soft bucket on the belt. I designed it to go halfway down to the floor so a window cleaner would be able to dip a 36-inch window washer inside the bucket, down through the tubing. This allowed for soaking a larger portion of the window washer. I made one prototype, and I used it as a demonstration prop in my seminars around the world. At the window cleaning convention in Singapore, there was a Japanese window cleaner who insisted on buying the prototype. He was so convincing that I sold it to him.

Just a side note and a reminder: inventing new products requires extensive planning and work. In order to manufacturer the bucket stand, I had to invent many different tools and jigs. However, this is where my experience in fabrication and welding came in handy. The high bucket stand is made up of a large number of parts, all of which are made in-house in the U.S., something we are very proud of at Sörbo Products.

"The best formula for window cleaning is Sörbo." Our swivel model from an ad in the mid-1990s.

Window cleaning seminar during the mid-'90s.

1997: Introducing the Sörbo Leif Cart

Winnie at a trade show in 1997.

In 1997, we were already cleaning windows with our Quadropod, the high bucket stand. During those years, my brother, Leif, periodically came over from Sweden and worked for our company. Eventually, he started cleaning storefront windows in Falun, Sweden. That's when he invented the Sörbo Leif Cart. A few years later, he offered me the option to market his rolling bucket stand.

Because we already manufactured the Quadropod, with the round bucket, I realized there was a need for a rectangular bucket. So, I redesigned it and made it wider for the big bucket. I also made it a lot lighter. My brother's idea, along with my improvements, turned out to be a very popular design for storefront windows that required more water. I named it the wet system because we designed it in such a way that it never spills water. The bucket swivels, so the water level remains balanced while moving. A window cleaner can roll it up and down stairways without spilling a drop of water. We named it after my twin brother, Leif. As with my other inventions, this rolling bucket stand needed a lot of different tooling, so I built a bending machine, and I also had to design a special punch press. The Leif Cart was all made in my welding shop. By fabricating the cart myself, I reduced a lot of the cost. Through the years, I have saved a tremendous amount of money because I have fabricated most of the equipment myself. I am guessing I have saved our company about $200,000.

1997: Improving the Scrubber Sleeve

I had been using different companies' scrubber sleeves for many years, but I realized it took a lot of pressure to remove the dirt from the window. So, I came up with a new design for our own scrubber sleeves. Instead of sewing it flat on each edge, I put one stitch in the middle of the scrubber material. That simple change turned out to be very efficient. From that point on, our scrubber sleeves became very flexible. Now, window washers using our scrubber sleeves did not need to apply as much pressure as before to clean their windows. As of 2023, we now offer the famous Grizzly Scrubber Sleeve.

1998: Inventing the Sörbo Fast-release. Patented, 1998

Through the years, a few different fast-release handles have been developed. All of them were designed to slide the handle all the way out to the end of the channel before you could remove it. In 1994, when I invented the first plastic end-plugged squeegee, the 3 × 4 adjustable Cobra channel, I had a problem. The end plugs stopped the handle from coming off. I decided to invent a new type of fast-release that opened up so a window cleaner could take it off anywhere along the channel. I also wanted to have easier access to the fast-release mechanism itself, so I invented a totally new design. I placed the leveler that releases the pressure underneath the upper jaw and attached it to the lower jaw. If you watch the YouTube videos, you can see that this new handle became the fastest-release handle on the market. Today, you can see my idea is widely used.

I also incorporated a stainless steel bar on top of the upper jaw, especially for high-rise window cleaning, so a window cleaner could attach the safety line. The old way was to hook it up to the handle grip. However, if you used a short extension pole, this was not possible. Therefore, I came up with this new attachment for the safety line. This allows a window cleaner to have an extension pole tip in the handle. This is also a safe way, if you do extension pole work, to attach the safety line to the extension pole at the top. This also prevents the squeegee from falling all the way down to the ground.

Sometimes, when I was working in between tree branches, the squeegee would fall off and almost hit my face. This was dangerous. Now, if a window cleaner loses control of the handle, it only falls as far as a safety line allows. When I developed this new handle, there wasn't much color in the window cleaning industry. The common color was black handles. So I decided to brighten up the industry and came out with the first three-color squeegee handle. I came up with yellow, purple, and black, and a gray safety plate on top for the safety line. This became a big hit, and it was the beginning of multicolored tools. Pretty soon, the whole window cleaning market started to be more colorful.

Last year, we came up with a new blue color that was very popular. Our squeegee handles are universal, and they fit all the squeegees on the market. All a window cleaner has to do is tighten the brass screw underneath the lower jaw and set it to a different thickness. Our handles even work on brass and stainless steel squeegees, which are made very rugged for a long life and designed for professionals.

But going back to the manufacturing of this new handle, a friend of mine knew a guy who had a machine shop in Mexico City. This guy would make the tooling for industrial and manufacturing molds. I met with both of them, and we discussed my new fast-release handle project. They promised to deliver a plastic injection mold in six months. Eighteen months later, the project was still incomplete. I decided to fly down to Mexico City to their shop to see for myself what was going on. At the same time, my Winnie flew to the Philippines to work with our school ministry. When I arrived at Mexico City Airport, I was immediately surrounded by taxi drivers. One of them just grabbed my luggage and started to walk toward his vehicle. He was pointing in the direction where he had parked his car. He had parked on a side street. Something did not feel right about the situation. When I came to his car, I spotted an old Volkswagen "Bug" with only one front seat for the driver. Although things seemed a bit fishy, I jumped into the back seat, stretching my legs all the way up to the front of the passenger side. The ride was okay, but the windows were broken, and the car had seen its best days.

When I arrived at the place where I was going to spend the night, which belonged to a real estate friend of mine from Palm Springs, Tom, he started screaming at the driver. "You blankety, blank, blank, bandit!"

I later found out that this was a transportation company that was stealing business from the government's taxi drivers. Anyway, everything was intact, and I got there safely. The next morning, Tom took me to a hotel in downtown Mexico City, where I would stay for the remainder of my time there. The following day, I met the owner of the machine shop for the first time. He had seven employees. I told him, "You have to stop everything you're working on and concentrate on my tooling!" So he did.

I realized he was a very nice man, so the first thing I did was go out and purchase chocolate, candies, Mexican pastries, and soda pops. I put a table in the middle of the shop to treat all of the workers. I figured that sugar would get them working faster. They were really happy to get so many goodies.

I told the owner, "I am going to help you, and I'm not going back home until these molds are finished!" I worked with the owner and his employees every day for two weeks.

Thankfully, I was staying in a very nice hotel in downtown Mexico City. One Saturday, I decided to do a little sightseeing, so I started to walk down the main streets. Suddenly, five Mexican guys surrounded me right there on the walkway. I could smell alcohol on them. I knew they were up to something bad. Luckily, they were not very big guys, and I was a lot taller than them. From my experience during my fighting days, I knew what to do. I hit them all in the face, and they fell in every direction. Before they had a chance to get up, I started to walk really fast down the street. I ran into a police officer and told him about the situation, but he didn't do anything. Looking back, I think he was probably involved. I crossed the street and walked into a shopping center that ran parallel to the entire street. So I kept walking through the center all the way back to the entrance of the hotel where I was staying. I went up to my room, took off all the gold chains and rings I was wearing, and put them into the safe.

After that, I went back down to the street and took a walk in the opposite direction. As I was walking, I passed a young man cleaning the windows of a storefront. I had given window cleaning seminars in a few cities in Mexico, but I had never met a window cleaner at work. So I stopped to watch him. To wet the window, I noticed he had a rusty metal can that he filled up with water from the water spigot. Then, he would walk back to the window and throw the water on the glass. He was using a very old, worn-out floor squeegee. Our distributors told me we never got a lot of sales in Mexico because Sörbo is such a high-quality, top-of-the-line product that people would steal them whenever they had the chance. That's why, in Mexico, they continue to sell the standard squeegees. But anyway, it turned out to be a good day.

On Monday morning, I went back to the shop owner. He was very nice, and he had a brother who was the company's salesperson. The brother showed me around town in his car. He had a young lady riding with him every time he took me for a ride. I was under the impression she was his wife. I was wrong. He explained to me that the young lady was his concubine. His wife was home taking care of the house and the kids. I discovered that this was a common practice.

Another thing I noticed during my time in Mexico was that young people were standing and kissing one another, here and there, out in public. To me, it was a little weird. I asked the driver what was going on with all this kissing everywhere on the streets. He told me that young couples did it to show that they were free to do whatever they pleased. I had never seen anything like it at home in America. I mean, these were no short kisses; it was like they were a form of life support.

Thankfully, in two weeks, the tooling project was done, and I flew back to California. A week later, the tooling was shipped to our company in California, and we were ready to produce of the new Sörbo Fast-release handles.

1998: Sörbo Products First Million-Dollar Order

In 1998, one of the biggest companies in the cleaning industry asked me to make them a custom squeegee. We have been to many trade shows throughout the years, and I have met many owners of big companies. Based on my academic background, you would never have predicted that I would have become Sörbo, the great businessman! Actually, I do not consider myself a businessman. I am a professional window cleaner who became one of the most successful inventors in the industry. Because of my experience in window cleaning, one thing I became very good at was demonstrating the products I invented. Every year at the ISSA trade show, I had large crowds watching me demonstrate how to properly use my new inventions. At one of the ISSA shows, a very well-known company that had never carried a commercial squeegee in their product line wanted to have a meeting regarding our product line. Wow!

We came home from the show very excited. Three of their sales reps in charge of marketing came to our little shop with a serious proposal. They had noticed throughout the years the many products I had invented. They asked me to make a special squeegee for them. I almost fell off the chair when they told me that their first order would be for $1,250,000.00. I said there was no way in the world we could make enough products in our little shop. However, they assured me that if we signed this contract, I would be able to acquire a loan from any bank for enough capital to build a factory.

We had a few meetings after that. I went to their headquarters for meetings, and finally, we all agreed to start the project. The pricing was okay. They asked me to calculate the packaging and the weight. I did all the prints for all the packaging and the weight for each pallet. It took me months to do it, and finally we were going to have a meeting at the Beverly Hills Hilton to finish up and sign the contract.

I arrived and met three of the sales representatives from this big corporation, and they wanted to talk about the pricing. "We already discussed that," I said.

"Yes, we did, but it is still a bit too high," they said.

They actually told me they had new numbers to show me. When I looked at the numbers, they were not acceptable to me. They kept telling me that this deal was going to be making me a lot of money because of the volume. I couldn't see any point in continuing.

I realized that they did not understand, or maybe they didn't want to understand, that Sörbo Products was a high-performance product line for professional commercial window cleaners.

They were going to try to compete with the standard squeegee lines, so they were trying to get the price per unit down, hoping to make up the difference through the sheer volume of sales. I made it clear that we were not a homeowner product line. We did not exist to compete with the standard household or low-end squeegees made in countries like China. Our target customers were professional and industrial window cleaners. Not one component in any of our products was made in China. We made everything in-house in the United States. I suggested they take their idea somewhere else. I could see by the look on their faces that they didn't expect that answer.

I realized later on that it was the right decision. I said to Winnie, "We can't even keep up with the orders we have right now!"

So, I praise the Lord that this deal never went through. But I never thought in my wildest dreams that somebody would place an order for $1,250.000 with us. I have been Blessed that I wasn't crazy about money and fame. Like I said, I'm a professional window cleaner and an inventor. That is my greatest joy. I look forward to inventing more efficient tools for window cleaners so they can be successful and make enough money to provide for their families. I look forward to helping window cleaners reduce the amount of labor they have to do each day. This is worth more than all the money in the world. I have proven that over and over again. One example of that is the squeegee blade trimmer, which allows a window cleaner to re-sharpen the squeegee rubber up to 12 times. If I were greedy, why would I be willing to lose the sale of a squeegee rubber every time a window cleaner sharpened one of our squeegee rubbers? If we didn't sell the Sörbo Docket, we would sell ten times more squeegee blades. (This is probably why we are the only company that markets a squeegee blade sharpener.)

Part V
Living My Testimony

1999: Facing the Biggest Miracle in My Life

In 1999, I experienced an event that I will never forget. My daughter Anette came home one day and told Winnie and me that we needed Jesus, and that she had become a born-again Christian. I said, "What is wrong with you?"

She tried to get us to attend a church service with her, but we refused. We did go with her on two other special holidays, together with my mom and my aunt, when they visited. A year later, our son, James, came home and talked to us about Jesus. I told him, "No more talk about your Jesus!"

However, when I looked at the church program he had with him, I realized that they had a lot of members at the church he attended. I said jokingly, "Maybe we should become members so we can sell our products to all the religious people in your church? Just kidding."

A year after James became a Christian, our youngest daughter, Mindi, came home telling us that she also had become a born-again Christian! I got so upset I called my mom in Sweden. I told her that our children were going crazy coming home proclaiming to be Christians, one after another. "What am I going to do?" I asked.

She said, "Don't worry. It will go away. It's one of those things young people do."

So I said, "Okay, thank you Mom."

Mindi did not push her religion on us. She would just close the door to her room when she came home. We found out later that she was reading the Bible and praying for us.

In 1999, Winnie surprised me with the news that Mindi was going to get married in three months' time. She also told me that Mindi and her fiancé, Bart, were inviting us to church. I said, "You go. I don't want to go."

Winnie said, "You have never spent any time with your daughter. You have never been to a ball game. You've never taken her to school. You have never done anything with her because you have always been busy working and inventing. You have the opportunity to spend some time with her these next three months. After that, she will be out of the house and married."

Winnie's words made me start to feel guilty, so I agreed to go. I felt very uncomfortable going to church. When we first visited Calvary Chapel in Cathedral City, California, I looked at all the people there, and a lot of them were younger adults. This was in December, and they had a candlelight service. After the service, when we were all outside the church, Mindi asked me, "Dad, what did you think about the sermon?"

"I don't know," I said because I didn't want to listen.

"Do you think you will come back to church?" she asked me.

I said, "No!"

This took place in December of 1999. In February 2000, Mindi and her Bart invited us again. To this day, I still don't understand or remember why I went.

At that time, Mindi and Bart had joined Palm Springs Community Church and were running their coffeehouse every Friday night. I agreed to go to church. When we arrived on Sunday morning, I met a bunch of very friendly people. The first members to greet us were Jack Young and his wife, Harriet. We were also greeted by Barbara and Wendell Veith. There were many other people who welcomed us to church that morning. The service started, and this time, I listened to Pastor Keith Newsome. As he spoke, I sat carefully listening and I heard things that I had never heard before.

Pastor Keith said, "God loves you, and if you ask for forgiveness, He will forgive all your sins."

I did not have to read a Bible to know that I was a sinner. I had a truckload of sins I had piled up over the years. But Pastor Keith said something else I had never heard before. He said, "You can have eternal life." He explained that God was going to create a new heaven and a new earth, and we would one day live here on this new earth forever and ever.

At that moment, I had a flashback. I was thinking back through all the years when I would sometimes find myself looking around, asking myself, "What is the meaning of my life? Is this all there is? Working, having a hangover, and then just dying?"

I remember my mom telling me, "When you die, you just go to sleep and there is nothing after that."

I thought about 1988, six years earlier, when I was struggling with addiction, and about the time God spoke to me and set me free from that terrible addiction. A couple of times, I'd even wanted to end my life. I was a workaholic who was working all the time. My mom and dad always told us, "When you get a job, never stay home even if you get sick, and never jump around from job to job."

I didn't know back then what I was looking for, but on that Sunday morning, as Pastor Keith preached, I realized that this is what I had been missing all my life! Can you imagine, even when God spoke to me six years earlier, I didn't want anything to do with Him? All those years I'd wasted running away and ignoring Him. But now it was clear why He had surrounded me with three Christian children. It is amazing how stupid and hardheaded I was! Now, here I was, getting an invitation to start a new and eternal life. And it didn't cost me anything! It was free! I read the sinner's prayer with everybody else who responded to Pastor Keith's message. While I was sitting there in the pew, I said in my mind, *Lord, if what Pastor Keith is saying is true, I want to live for You for the rest of my life.*

As soon as I said that, I felt like a multitude of weights had come off my shoulders. It was the most joyful feeling I've ever felt! I felt such a relief. I felt so free like I was flying! Tears started running down my cheeks. This was something I'd never experienced growing up. It was like a flood coming out of my eyes. I felt such a joy, I couldn't fully explain this new feeling.

Then Pastor Keith said, "For those of you who have accepted Jesus Christ into your heart, come on up so the elders can pray for you."

I kept weeping, and I still don't know to this day how I got up to the altar. I needed windshield wipers. *Order Sörbo five-inch squeegees in order to see,* I thought to myself.

Well, I ended up in front of Pastor Keith, and I looked at him with my wet face, and I asked, "Pastor, do you think I can get forgiveness?"

He said, "Young man, you would not be up here if you had not gotten saved."

And then he prayed over me. When he was done praying, I looked to my left, and there was Winnie standing in front of an elder, also weeping. There were about a half-dozen people who got saved that morning. After the prayer, Pastor Keith invited me to come to his office the next day. He said, "I can explain what happened today."

So that's what I did. I knew I was changed. I was feeling like a new person, thanks to Jesus, who had saved my life six years earlier so I could be redeemed that day! When I walked out of the church that day, everything looked so different. Everything was so bright, nice, and clean. It was miraculous!

Our daughter Mindi was working at the back of the church with the children. She was quickly told by her friends that her mom and dad had accepted Jesus into their hearts. She came out weeping. Today, I am so grateful for her and her husband, Bart, and their church members who had been praying for us for so long.

On Monday, I went to see Pastor Keith, and he prayed for me and explained to me what had happened the day before. He took time to explain things in the Bible and read some verses from the Bible that he gave me. The next weekend, I felt like I should do something for God since He had been so nice to save me. I noticed the windows of the church were very dirty. As a window cleaner, that's the first thing you see when you walk into a building. So, I asked Pastor Keith if I could clean the church windows. He was really happy because he said that nobody had cleaned the church windows since he had become the pastor of the church. Since I had a manufacturing company that made window cleaning equipment, it made sense.

So the next Saturday morning, I cleaned the windows. I was almost finished when one of the elders came out to greet me. His name was Bob Olson, and he was a very nice man. He and his wife, Lorraine, were snowbirds from Minnesota who came to the Coachella Valley every winter to their second home.

He said, "We have a men's Bible study here every Saturday morning. Would you like to take a little break and come in and join us?"

"I don't know if I have time. I have other things to do on the weekends," I said.

I was thinking to myself, *I'm born again. Isn't that enough? Do I really have to be so involved?*

Then he said, "We have a great cook here. His name is Bob McDonald. He makes a fabulous breakfast, which includes scrambled eggs, sausage, and waffles with strawberries and whipped cream. Why don't you just come in and enjoy a good breakfast? Besides, it's free!"

"I'll be right there!" I said.

The man teaching was Wendell Veith. He explained the Bible so clearly. It wasn't difficult to understand. I really enjoyed listening to him teach. It was like listening to a history teacher who explained things that have been going on in our world since the beginning of time up to the present and even about events to come. For the first time in my life, I realized the Scriptures were very interesting. After that first Bible study, I never missed the opportunity to go to Bible studies. I even went to other Bible studies in the middle of the week, looking to learn as much as I could about my new faith.

I learn more by listening to people teach because I have such a hard time remembering anything I have to read. I have never been a strong reader. When I listen to a good teacher, I remember most of what they say, so I learn more.

2000: Sören Samuelsson Will Be Baptized

Palm Springs Community Church had two buildings, one on each side of the street. The larger church building was built in 1959. The smaller building on the north side of the street was a historic building constructed in the 1920s. That is the church building where I got saved, and it is still there today. A few years after I was saved, the congregation decided to sell the big church in Palm Springs. Two weeks after the building was sold, our daughter and Bart got married in that church. Two years later, on February 10, 2002, I got baptized. I remember telling Winnie about it because she was in the Philippines. She asked if I could wait until she came home. But I said, "I can't wait. I don't know when the next baptism will be. I want to get baptized right away."

Getting ready for my baptism in 2002.

Rising anew from my baptism.

I'll never forget when Pastor Keith and Pastor Jack Merenda baptized me. When I came up out of the water, I had a vision of myself standing in front of a large crowd of people. I told my wife I couldn't understand what it meant. Sometime later, Winnie felt a strong sense to go to the Philippines and build schools in the villages where indigenous people live. Our company was doing well enough for us to help the poor in her country. I changed my whole outlook in my personal life. Six months later, when I was leaving the Sunday morning Bible study at our church in Palm Springs, I realized the streets were closed off and that there were bikers everywhere. This was because of the biker event called American Heat, which was held in Palm Springs. I made a U-turn, parked the van in the church parking lot, and walked back to where the bikers were. The first booth I walked up to had a sign that read "Christian Motorcyclists Association." There were some really rough-looking guys standing there. I was thinking, *These guys can't be Christians.*

The way they looked and dressed, I'd never seen a Christian biker in my life. I almost hesitated to go up and talk to them, but I finally did. To my great surprise, they were on fire for the Lord! I never knew that a biker who looked like that could be a Christian, but these guys were very much so, and we quickly became friends.

"Why don't you come ride with us? We have one hundred and eighty thousand CMA members all over the world," they said.

"I would love to!" I said. "But I don't have a bike right now. As soon as I get one, I will join your organization."

So, I gathered all the information. When I got home that afternoon, I told Winnie about my experience. I asked her, even though I knew it was impossible, "Do you think I can buy a Harley?"

She said, "You know very well that we can't afford that right now."

"I know that," I said, "but even if you would have said yes, I would not have bought one anyway!" I laughed.

"I have learned from the Bible that sometimes God does give us what we pray for. So I'll start praying for a Harley," I told her. She looked at me with a doubtful grin.

I asked Jesus to change Winnie's heart about buying a motorcycle and to make it possible for me to join the CMA. Like a child waiting for Christmas, I couldn't wait to ride with these guys.

2000: The Sörbo Silverado Economy Squeegee is Born

My innovation award from 2000, received at The Interclean Show in Amsterdam — the largest convention in the world for our industry.

In 2000, I designed my fourth wide-body squeegee model. I called it the Silverado. This was a descendent of the Sörbo 3 × 4 Adjustable Wide-Body squeegee. I decided to develop a lower-cost wide-body squeegee. The design came from the Cobra channel. I simply removed the plastic end plugs and cut it 90 degrees at each end. This channel was produced in sizes that ranged from 12 to 36 inches. It was sold with the famous Sörbo silicone squeegee blade, excellent for straight strokes and fanning. The Silverado became the economy line squeegee that we sold to customers who were just starting in the window washing industry and had a limited budget or in countries where the economy could not support our higher-end products. This was the fourth model that we developed. The Silverado's low cost was very well received by the window cleaners.

2001: Sörbo Sales Increase Tremendously

We needed one more 36-inch mold. The cost of the mold was $40,000, an amount we could not afford at the time. So I said to Winnie, "Let's pray that God will find a way to provide $40,000."

After I became a born-again Christian, I started to tell my family about Jesus. My Aunt Gunvor, in New York, was the first person in our family to whom I witnessed. I knew she and my uncle were members of the Catholic Church. A few years earlier, my uncle had passed away from cancer. However, at the time of his passing, we were not saved, and we didn't know anything about Jesus. But now my aunt had been by herself for many years, and she had a friendly relationship with an older man, Michael.

We met him when we traveled around the United States in 1973. Through the years, I had been talking to my Aunt Gunvor about Jesus. One Sunday in February, we had a long talk about heaven and how to get there. I explained to her that if she asked for forgiveness and believed Jesus had died for her sins, she would be saved, as stated in the Gospel of John 3:16–18.

For God so loved the world that he gave his one and only
Son, that whoever believes in him shall not perish but have
eternal life.17 For God did not send his Son into the world
to condemn the world, but to save the world through him.
(John 3:16–17)

After the conversation, I was so excited. I told Winnie, "I think Aunty is getting closer to believing in Jesus!"

That evening at around 7 o'clock, my aunt called back, and she asked for prayer for her friend Michael, who had just suffered a heart attack. She was very worried that she would lose her friend, and she wanted us to pray for him. She had told us before that he had already had half a dozen heart attacks. I was just a baby in Christ at that time, so together, we prayed. I realized her faith had grown in the few months I'd been talking to her about Jesus. It was an awesome feeling! Together, we prayed for Michael's healing, and that evening, my wife and I gave thanks to the Lord for opening Aunt Gunvor's heart.

Monday morning, very early, the telephone rang. A friend of my aunt called, and she told me she was calling about my aunt. I said, "Yeah, we talked to her about Michael last night. How is he doing?"

"He is doing fine," she said, "but your Aunt Gunvor died last night."

I couldn't believe it!

We hung up, and I told Winnie what had happened. This came as a big shock to both of us. I immediately called my mom in Sweden. It was still evening over there; they are nine hours ahead of our local time. I told my mom, "Something terrible happened. Your sister passed away last night."

The first thing she said was, "Is this some kind of preaching like you did when you became a Christian?"

I suppose in her confusion, she didn't want to believe what I'd said. Then she started weeping. She said she couldn't believe it was true. After a long conversation, we hung up. She said she was going to arrange to come to the United States for my aunt's funeral services. So, Mom and Dad were going to fly to New York, and later on, my brother, Leif, decided to come too. They all wanted to help me, so I started to pray for safe travel. I asked God to comfort my family members who were coming from Sweden.

I said to Winnie, "I'm the only relative my aunt had in America."

I called for an airline ticket to New York. Then I realized that I had to go there and sell my aunt's house during a very bad recession. I thought the recession would make it difficult to sell the house, so Winnie and I started to pray that God would help me sell the home quickly.

I was able to get a flight in three days. Ted Jaroszewsky, a close friend of my Uncle Walter, picked me up at Albany International Airport and took me to the police station in Catskill to pick up the key to my aunt's house. The police officer expressed his sorrow for what had happened. Then he asked, "What are you going to do with the house? Are you going to sell it?"

"Yes," I responded.

"I want to buy it!" he said.

"Praise the Lord!" I exclaimed.

He was surprised by my response. I told him that I had prayed to God to help me sell the house, and now here the house was just about sold before I even had a chance to get it ready for sellers to view. God had answered our prayers.

The house needed a good cleaning, and I wanted it to be ready before my mom, dad, and brother showed up the next day. That evening, I received a telephone call from my pastor, Keith Newsome. He offered to pray for me. I told him I was grateful for his call and for the prayer. I really needed it.

I spent the whole day cleaning. The next evening came quickly, and suddenly, I realized I had to go to the train station to pick up my family. I wasn't even finished cleaning. I wanted my family, especially my dad, to feel good when they came because I knew that he must have had a stressful time traveling from Sweden. I prayed, "Lord, make more time for me so I can finish the cleaning."

I arrived at the train station, but they were not on the train. I found out the train was late because of the snow in New York City. The next train would be arriving in three hours. My prayers were answered again! I went back to the house and finished the cleaning job just in time.

After they arrived, we all came back to the house. I didn't hear any complaining about the way the house looked. Everyone had a discussion about how sad we were that my mom's sister had passed away. They also told me how great the trip had turned out to be. I said, "My Friend must have arranged everything."

If you remember, earlier in my book, I told you how upset my dad could get whenever I talked about God. So, I chose my words a little more carefully that day. Especially now that he was many years older.

They told me they had got tickets at a discount, and they had been able to get flights in two days. However, they had arrived late at Kennedy Airport due to the weather. That was okay, though, because they took the next Amtrak up to Catskill.

They said, "The Amtrak conductor took care of all of us the whole way like we were babies. We felt so safe. We couldn't believe how nice he was."

From my point of view, I could tell that "Somebody" was looking out for them. During our discussion, an announcement came over the radio warning about a snowstorm coming into Catskill. That would have been a catastrophic situation. I talked to my Friend and asked if He could delay the storm until they left in two weeks. My dad got upset because I was "talking" to God again. I didn't let that bother me.

Their tickets were only good for two weeks. My mom said, "We're never going to be able to finish this big job before we have to leave!"

So I said, "We will pray that God will help us. He saved my life, and set me free from my addiction. He can surely shorten the time it takes so we can manage to do what we're supposed to do."

Right there in the living room, I led us in prayer. Well, just a few days before they were going to leave, everything was done. Mom, Dad, and my brother were all amazed at how easily everything had worked out. They couldn't understand it. I told them it was because we prayed, and to my surprise, my brother, Leif, said, "It looks like those prayers work!"

It was really good news to my ears to hear him say that.

2001: Are You A Pastor?

On February 27, 2001, we had the funeral service for my aunt. I'd been trying to write something down to say at the funeral. I had a song that I included my aunt's name in, but I couldn't concentrate. I thought, *I'm not going to write anything in advance. I'm going to let the Holy Spirit take care of my mouth when I speak at the funeral.*

I'm paraphrasing, but some time before, I had heard that in the Bible, it is written, "Don't be worried about what you are going to say. I will take care of your mouth." So, I relied on God. I don't remember what I said, but it must have been good because the priest asked me if I was a pastor.

Well, the next morning I took Mom, Dad, and my brother to the railroad station, and they took the Amtrak back to Kennedy Airport. As soon as my family left, I went back to the house. That evening, Ted called me and said he was worried about my family because 75 percent of the airlines were grounded in New York, where my mom and dad were going to be flying out of, back to Sweden. All of a sudden, it started to snow. It snowed all night and the next day as well. God had held back the snow the whole time we were there. Before I left, there was a foot of snow already. I called Ted, and I handed over Uncle Walter's car to him as a gift for helping us. When he came to pick me up to take me to Albany International Airport, he barely made it onto the driveway because it was covered with so much snow.

When I arrived at the airport, I figured my family would be in Sweden already. I called them, and my mom said the last miracle had taken place when they arrived in Finland. The flight was late because of a headwind from New York. They figured they would miss the train to Sweden. But my mom said that train was late too, so they made it home that night. She said it was the best trip they had ever had. I thought to myself, *God arranged the whole thing.*

I had problems leaving Albany. My flight was scheduled to leave at 9:15 a.m., but it left at 10:30 a.m. I prayed again that I would make it for the next flight. When I landed at Newark Liberty International Airport, it was 12:45 p.m. My connecting flight had been scheduled to leave at 12:20 p.m. When I arrived at the gate, there were no passengers there. I looked at the screen, and to my surprise, the plane was late. It was scheduled to depart from a different gate in 15 minutes! I started running and got to the gate in time. It was the last miracle of my long trip. Many of you who are reading this can relate to what I am sharing because your eyes are open, and you understand exactly what God is doing. Amen.

Well, my aunt's attorney helped us with all the legal documents concerning her will. The amazing fact is that my brother and I received $80,000, which we split in half. I got $40,000 cash, which was the exact amount we needed for the rubber molding. A week later, Winnie and I ordered the mold we had prayed for. I never dreamed that I would have experienced all these answered prayers. But then again, I'm not God.

I can assure you that our relationship with Jesus has helped me and my family to achieve everything we have. If I told you everything God has done for my business, for my family, and for me personally, you might not believe it. Maybe the only way you will place your trust in God, as I have, is if your eyes are open to His goodness and love for you and me.

2001: My Hidden Talent

A year had gone by since Winnie and I were saved. One day, Winnie told me she wanted to join the church choir. My response was, "You can do that if you like, but you won't catch me singing in a choir."

"But I want you to come!" she insisted.

"Honey, I couldn't even memorize one song!" I said. "You can go, but I'm staying home."

But Winnie is persistent, and she begged me to come with her. So, like the loving husband I am, I did.

At choir practice, I was lucky enough to sit beside a Swedish-born lady from Minnesota. So, I followed her and I was able to sound the same. The problem was that if she did not come to choir practice, I couldn't sing, so I just moved my mouth. After a year, Wendell, the choir director, told me that I had a good voice and he wanted me to sing a solo. I got so nervous I almost got diarrhea. I told him, "I'm sorry, but you know what? I can't memorize the song. So how can I sing?"

Wendell said, "You can read the text when you sing. Just give it a try."

Suddenly, I had a flashback. I remembered the time when my dad told me my singing was terrible and told me to be quiet. Now, here I was, being asked to sing a solo fifty years later! But then I remembered the vision God gave me when I got baptized. I was standing in front of a whole bunch of people. And I wondered if this had something to do with that prophecy.

In February of that same year, we were going to Florida for the IWCA trade show. I needed a sound system to demonstrate the use of our equipment. I went shopping for one, and when I got to the music store in Florida, they had a sale on a karaoke system. It seemed to me like it was God's plan to get me to sing. To make a long story short, I began to get into singing more and more, so I began buying background soundtracks from the Christian bookstore. I also recorded my own CDs on my computer. Through the years, I have recorded six CDs, which I sold at my concerts that I started a few years later; all the money went to our children's ministry in the Philippines.

2001: Improving the Sörbo End Clip Design.

The totally newly designed stainless steel end clips that I invented in 1989 were nothing like the clips in the standard squeegees at the time. Before our product came along, standard squeegee end clips were made of thin brass sheet metal. These wrapped around the squeegee rubber and pushed into the channel at each end. Because of the four adjustments in the channel, the space was very limited. So, I invented this new clip in the shape of a small boat. On the first design, the bottom of the end clip was flat. This caused some complaints from our customers. They told us that the rubber was slipping whenever the water was too soapy. We listened to the window cleaners and made a simple change, which solved the problem. We added two small bumps to the bottom of the end clips. This change prevented the wet rubber blade from slipping off the squeegee handle. We never had a complaint after that. I am grateful for the feedback we got from our customers.

2002: The Miracle and the Bicycle Key with the Blue Ribbon

In the spring of 2002, the Holy Spirit spoke to my heart. He said to me, "Sören, go home to your mother and father. Once you are there, for a week, pray with your mother and father every morning. Then go to the creek that you went fishing in when you were young. Take home a big fish every day of the week."

When I heard this thought in my mind, I panicked and I said to the Lord, "Lord, when I went fishing in the creek in my youth, I never caught a big fish. I only ever caught small bass. Suppose I pray with my parents and ask You to let me catch a large fish every morning and I come home empty-handed. Will they ever believe in You?"

I sensed the Lord telling me, "If you have faith and believe Me, you will catch a large fish every day."

And I said, "Lord, I do have faith in You!"

I purchased a plane ticket for Sweden, and I made plans to visit my parents for ten days. Then I called and surprised my mom and dad. I told them, "I'll be coming home to visit soon." I should tell you that the place where the Holy Spirit told me to fish for a week was a very small creek. It was no more than 15 feet wide, and ever since I was a kid, I had never got a big fish in that little creek. I had only ever caught small bass.

One week before I was scheduled to go and visit them, I was planning to tell them why I was going and what God had told me to do once I was there. So, the next Sunday, I told my mom and dad that while I was there, God wanted us to pray together every morning just before I went fishing. We were to ask God to allow me to catch a large fish every day. My father was not very happy with what I told them. "You and your God," he said.

I arrived a week later, and on the first morning, in spite of their hesitation and unhappy attitude, I prayed that God would grant me the opportunity to bring home a big fish from the little creek. I asked my dad if I could borrow his bicycle because it was about a 15-minute bike ride to the creek.

I was nervous. *Suppose it wasn't God who had spoken to me?*

I was praying the whole time, "Please don't fail me, Lord!"

When I got to the small creek, I parked the bike in between two trees. I removed the lock and put it around the wheel. Then I put the key, which had a blue ribbon tied to it, in my pocket. One can only walk beside the creek for about a mile. This one-mile fishing spot ran between two bridges. This was the best place to fish if I was going to bring home a catch.

Well, as I started fishing, I prayed, "Lord, You have to provide me with a big fish now!"

I was casting my spinner as I walked along on my way up the creek, thinking what Mom and Dad would say if I came home without a fish. Or, what would they say if I came home with a lot of fish? When I had walked and cast my line for about one-third of the way up the creek, suddenly something bit on the spinner, and I pulled really hard! I could feel the resistance of a big fish because the fishing line was being stretched very hard. I started reeling it in as fast as I could. Praise the Lord! It was a large carp! In all the years I had come fishing here after school, I had only ever caught bass. This was a carp that measured almost 24 inches! I got so excited that I shouted, "Thank you, Lord!"

I couldn't wait to get home to show my mom and dad how God had answered my morning prayer. Quickly, I gathered all my fishing gear, unlocked my dad's bike, and pedaled back home as fast as I could. I don't think I ever rode a bike so fast and with as much excitement as I did that day.

When I got home, my mom and dad were so surprised to see me return so soon. When they saw my catch, they immediately got their camera and took photos of me and the big fish I had caught that morning. They took out the measuring tape to measure its length. They wanted to know exactly how long the fish was. When they realized how long the fish was, they were filled with excitement and joy.

Well, God told me I was going to catch a large fish every day that week, and this was only the first day. So, on Tuesday morning, I prayed with my parents again, and then I peddled out to the little creek again.

I said to myself, *How am I going to top yesterday's catch?*

I had a difficult time believing that there was room for anymore large fish in the little creek. I locked my father's bike in the same spot as before, and I put the key in my pocket. Then, I prayed that I would get another fish. When I passed the place where I had caught that big fish the day before, I began to feel nervous, but I kept throwing the spinner as I walked along the narrow creek. About two-thirds of the way up the little stream, I felt another strong bite again! I immediately pulled on the fishing pole really hard to secure the fish.

I shouted, "Praise the Lord!"

God told me I would catch a fish every day, and this was one of them.

Cleaning my catch in Vassbo, Sweden.

Setting up for a picture of another catch in Vassbo.

My mother, admiring another catch of the day.

Fishing in Vassbo.

I was reeling in the big catch as fast as I could. I did not want to lose whatever it was I had caught. I could feel the fish was a good size, and wouldn't you know it, it was the same size as the one I had got the day before! After reeling in my second catch of the week, I immediately put all my fishing gear together, ran down to the bicycle, and pedaled home, thanking the Lord the entire way.

When I arrived with a second big catch in two consecutive days, my mom and dad seemed more surprised than the day before. My faith was strengthened. My mom prepared a wonderful dinner using the fish I had caught the day before. I have always loved the egg gravy my mom made with hard-boiled eggs in it. It's so creamy. We had fresh carp with potatoes and gravy for dinner that night. It was the best meal I had shared with my parents in a long time.

Now Mom had one more to clean and put in the refrigerator. I was amazed myself, and I said to my mom and dad, "Let's do it again tomorrow morning!"

Wednesday, I prayed again, asking God to allow me to get a big fish. Then, I pedaled all the way out to the small creek and started fishing again. About half the way up the creek, I got another big bite again! I hauled in one more big fish about the same size as the first two. I said to myself, *This is really working. Maybe I should try to get one more.*

So I continued up the stream, and — wouldn't you know? — I got another bite again! This one was a little bit smaller than the first three, but my goodness, I got two that day! This was starting to feel crazy. But then I started thinking that maybe I shouldn't have kept fishing. *What is going to happen tomorrow? I wondered. Maybe the second fish was meant for tomorrow. Lord, forgive me for being greedy.*

That morning, I showed up with two big fish coming home, and again, the camera came out, and the camcorder also. That night, we had fish for dinner again, and, believe me, my faith was growing with every fish I caught. We all liked fish, and now we had two more. My mom had to put one in the freezer. We actually ate fish every day that week. I didn't mind, and now we had one extra.

That afternoon, we all went to the nursery on the outskirts of town to buy flowers. My nephew was going to graduate from college. On Thursday morning, we all prayed again that I would catch a big fish. By now, my faith had grown so much that I brought my video camera to record the next fish I caught. This was starting to be a real miracle, and I wanted to record it so I would have proof of what God had done.

I arrived at the creek and put the bike behind the trees to hide it from the traffic crossing the bridge, but now I couldn't find the key for the bicycle lock that I kept in my pocket. I started looking on the ground, in the grass around where the bike was parked, and I couldn't find it! "Lord, I have to find the key; otherwise my dad is going to be very upset when I come home," I prayed as I looked for the key.

My dad really had a bad temper, and when something went wrong, he would get very upset. I really needed to find that key. As I crawled around on the ground trying to find the key, I kept saying, "Lord, I need to find the key."

I sensed the Lord say to me, "You will find the key, Sören." I kept crawling around in the grass around the bike, but I didn't find the key.

In my frustration, I said, "Where is it, Lord? You told me I would find the key." Suddenly, I remembered that somewhere in the Bible it says something like, "It is not my timing; it is God's timing, and the two are very different." I also remember hearing that the Bible says for God, one day is like 1,000 years, and 1,000 years is like one day. I have learned from experience that God can be late when I pray for help, but He is never too late. God tests us a lot. So, on the way home, I prayed for my dad not to get angry when I told him that I had lost the key to his bike lock.

I started to walk up the creek, casting out the spinner, and this day, I came up three-quarters of the way to the second bridge that crossed the creek. I was almost up to the next bridge. I had my video camera running every time I stopped. I said, "I need to have another fish, Lord!"

Almost as soon as the words came out of my mouth, I felt another big tug on my line. I pulled the line hard, and I started to reel it in. This section of the creek was very swampy. When I got the fish to the shoreline, about halfway up, the fish came off the spinner, and it ended up on the bank of the small creek. I threw the fishing pole aside and launched myself forward like a torpedo. I landed on my stomach in that swampy water, but I got a hold of the fish before it fell into the water again. I grabbed the big fish and threw it up behind me, out into the field where the cows and the horses were walking around. That big fish went flying through the air and landed around 25 feet from where I was. It was a good thing it didn't land in the cow dung. The most important thing was that I didn't lose it. "Thank you, Lord!" I said.

I grabbed my video equipment and started pedaling home. When I got home, Mom and Dad started taking pictures and measuring the fish to determine how long it was. By now, they had gotten used to this happening every day. We had been eating fish every day, and the refrigerator had started to get filled up with fish. The amazing thing was that the last fish I'd caught was bigger than the other ones that had come before. But now I had to tell my dad the bad news.

I said, "Dad, I have to tell you something you are not going to like. I lost your bicycle key."

To my surprise, he didn't get upset. I exclaimed in a loud voice, "Thank you, Lord!"

My father asked me, "Why do you scream like that?"

I explained to him that I had prayed before I'd left the creek that he would not get upset when I told him I had lost the key to his bike. He was not upset, so I was thanking God for answering my prayer.

My dad looked at me and said in a pessimistic tone, "You and your God."

If you are still reading this book, I can imagine that some of you have already experienced the power of the Holy Spirit in a similar way as I have. If that is true, I know you are enjoying reading my book. But maybe there are some who have not experienced anything like I have since God saved me. Never forget that the Bible contains an open invitation. If you ask for it, you will receive salvation. Don't for a minute think that I could say and do what I'm doing if God had not filled my inner man with His Spirit. I am not the man I was before God saved me. Before I was born again, I was bad. It's very easy to be mean and bad, but to do what I do now when I speak about Jesus, I would never have been able to do before His Spirit came in and gave me His power to be His witness. That has been the difference in my life. You have to ask God to look at your heart. He doesn't care how you say it.

Simply say, "Jesus, come into my heart, and I will live for You for the rest of my life. Amen." If you do this, you will receive a new spiritual birthday, marking you for eternal life.

Anyway, back to my incredible fishing story. I told Dad that God had said to me that we would find the key but that He hadn't told me where and when. I told him I believed we would find it. I also told him not to worry if we did not find the key. I was willing and able to buy him a new bike. The next day, Friday, we prayed, and I went fishing just as I had done the previous four days, and I got one more big fish. That completed the prophecy. Although my mom, my dad, and I had witnessed a miracle that week, they did not become Christians right away. Many years passed before I was able to lead my mom and dad to Christ. And one of the reasons is that they were really good people, and they didn't think they were sinners. My mom said, "Well, I think we have been good, and besides that, I was baptized when I was a baby and therefore I should have eternal life."

If anyone tells you this, they are being totally misleading. To receive salvation, you have to be in the state of mind to choose for yourself. Nobody else can choose for you.

It was time for me to go back home to California, and we still hadn't found the key. Before I left, I reminded my dad that the Lord had told me we would find his key, but He hadn't told me where and when. When I got back home to California, I told Winnie the story, and she agreed that we had to trust the Lord. The days stretched on, and we forgot about that key. Then, three weeks later, we received an unexpected call from Mom. She told us she was using a speakerphone on the table so Dad could be right there, listening in on the call. My mom and dad always did everything together.

Then my mom said, "You will never guess what happened!" Immediately, I said, "Yes I can! You found the key!"

My dad exclaimed to my mom, "How could he know that?"

I responded, "Dad, remember I said to you that God told me we would find the key, but He didn't say where and when."

Mom said, "You won't believe this!" and she told me how it had all happened: That day, my mom and dad went to buy flowers for the garden. It was now summer, and the days were much warmer. When they arrived at the nursery, they parked the car, went into the nursery, and started looking around at the flowers. My dad became concerned that the car was going to get too hot in the sun, so he went outside to move the car under the shade of a large tree near the parking lot exit. Then he went back into the nursery and continued to look at the flowers with Mom. When they were done shopping, my dad sat in the driver's seat, and my mom went to get into the passenger's seat. When she sat down, with her feet still on the ground, she couldn't believe her eyes. There, on the ground, in between her shoes, was Dad's bicycle key with the blue ribbon, lying on the ground. My mom was thunderstruck!

My dad noticed that something had happened, so he asked Mom, "What's wrong?"

In a surprised voice, my mom answered him, "I found your bicycle key with the blue ribbon!"

She repeated this to my dad at least three times. My dad thought she was going crazy. My mom thought the whole incident was kind of spooky. Like something out of a movie. She told me she had goosebumps all over her body.

I was so excited that I asked her, "What did you do?

She said, "We could barely believe our eyes! We were both so surprised, we had to go into the nursery to tell the manager what happened!"

"Did you tell him God told us three weeks earlier that you would find the key?" I asked her.

She said, "No! I didn't do that because it was too spooky."

This was the store where we had gone to buy flowers three weeks earlier for my nephew's graduation. The only conclusion I came to was that God had made me drop the key there just to complete the miracles and to show my mom and dad that He is real. The strange thing is that I had not walked up to the driveway when we were at the nursery. So, I suppose God plucked the key out of my pocket and put it in a safe place so nobody would pick it up, right at the entrance where the cars go in and out.

I will never forget that week. Neither did my mom and dad. I have told that miracle story in my concert ministry many times through the years. My daughter told me to write down all the miracles that had happened in my life, so I did.

However, the miracle of the fish and the key is nothing compared to what God did for me and in me. He saved my life so many times. And when I was 55 years old, He got the old man out of me. That is the biggest miracle. And most of my old friends can't believe their eyes.

Another miracle took place when my brother and his family came to visit us. A couple of days before they were going to go back to Sweden, my brother became very worried because they had miscalculated the date to fly back home. This miscalculation was going to cause them to miss their son's graduation. I told him we should pray and ask God to cause the graduation date to be changed. I said, "I believe God will listen to us. But then it is up to Him if He thinks it is best to grant us our request. But if you don't ask, then nothing will happen."

Just before we prayed, I asked my brother for a favor. I said, "When you return to Sweden, I would like you to call me if God answers our prayer."

He agreed. However, I did not hear from him regarding what had happened with our prayer about his son's graduation until a year later, when we went to Sweden to visit my mom and dad. While we were there, I remembered this, and I asked my brother, "Do you remember when we prayed that God would change the dates for Hanrik? You promised to tell me if God answered our prayer or not. What happened? Did God answer our prayer?"

He told me there had been a terrible storm that weekend, so the graduation had been moved forward to the following weekend. "That was not because of the prayer. It was because of the weather," he told me.

"That's how God works sometimes," I said.

It's like the story about that guy who was sitting on the roof in the middle of a tsunami, and the rescue crew came by in a boat and told the man they were there to rescue him. The guy said, "No, thank you. I'm relying on God."

Soon, a helicopter came by and lowered a basket to save him. Again, he said, "No, thank you. I'm relying on God."

After a while, the water level got so high that he drowned. When he arrived in heaven and met Jesus, he asked, "Why didn't You help me when I was praying?"

Jesus answered him, "I sent people on a boat to rescue you and you refused. Then I sent people in a helicopter, and you refused them too. Did you expect me to show up in person? I don't work that way."

God sends people to help us. Sometimes, the people He sends might even be angels. We often don't realize it until later on. For example, I remember there was a homeless guy outside a Circle K. He was begging for money. I asked him, "Are you hungry, sir?"

"Yes. Can you buy me a hot dog?" he said.

"I can do that for you," I said.

So I went into the store and made up a hot dog and a drink, and went out and handed it to him. He thanked me, and I went back into the store to buy some more stuff for myself. I was going to talk to him as soon as I got out of the store but, to my surprise, when I walked out of the store he was nowhere to be found. It was like he'd actually disappeared. I say this because the store was completely surrounded by empty lots and desert. There was no way that man had had a chance to walk far without me seeing him. I had only spent a couple of minutes in the store. I don't know if God was testing me, but it is things like this that increase your faith.

2003: Purchasing My Harley-Davidson Road King

Earlier, I mentioned that in 2001, I had started praying for a Harley-Davidson. Two years later, as if inspired by God, Winnie asked me, "When are you going to buy that Harley?"

I shouted, "Praise the Lord!"

This was on a Sunday. By Wednesday, I had a Harley Road King parked in my garage! I immediately called the local CMA chapter, but to my surprise, I discovered that this chapter had broken up. Some of the members had moved out of town. So, I joined the Riverside-San Bernardino chapter. That is when I got introduced to Bill Glass Ministries, which focused on people in prison. Well, I'd had a taste of prison myself, so I joined up with the guys and started doing rides up to Fresno, California, to preach the Gospel to the inmates.

There were about 33,000 inmates in surrounding prisons at that time, and through the years, I visited every single one of them. Some of my Christian brothers and sisters began talking about starting a chapter in Palm Springs. The crazy thing is that they wanted me to be the president. I said I couldn't do it because I had never done anything like that before. But God had other plans. In October of that year, we set up the CMA booth at the big motorcycle event, American Heat, in Palm Springs. We interacted and shared the Gospel of Jesus with bikers for two days. In that short time, 38 bikers signed up to be members. In spite of my lack of faith, the members were right. I became our chapter president and served for the next six years. I stepped down when I started the bikers' ministry in Sweden. I learned a lot through those years, like how to minister to rough bikers who have chosen the wrong road in this life. To later see them become born-again Christians brought me great joy. I probably mentioned this before, but there are about 180,000 bikers all over the world in this organization, whose headquarters is in Arkansas.

2006: We Needed One More Mold, Which Would Cost Another $40,000

I was almost embarrassed to ask the Lord for help again. We had been spending most of our profits on buying a lot of dies to stamp our stainless steel parts for the squeegees. On top of that, we were also paying for all our patents. The total for patents alone was close to $100,000. However, it was also during this time that we started having Bible studies for all the employees on Friday mornings. So I said to Winnie, "Let's pray that God will make a way to provide $40,000, again." We couldn't get enough rubber parts and we needed to increase production.

One early morning, when I was up at my friend's yard, standing in the back of the trailer loading up some material, I got a phone call from one of our master distributors. He said, "We had a meeting yesterday and we talked about how we can help your company. We decided to help you by sending $40,000 for our account in advance, which can be deducted from the orders we place with you in the future."

Well, you know me. I said, "Praise the Lord! Our prayer came true again!"

My buddy said, "What is happening?"

I told him that we had been praying for $40,000, and we had just received God's answer to our prayer through that phone call. This was Mats, my old school friend from Sweden. He looked at me and shook his head. He was not saved at that time, but after many years, I led him to Christ 45 minutes before he passed away.

If I told you all the things we have received through praying, you would probably not believe me. Still, I will share two more miracles with you. These just now came to my mind as I was writing this book.

Many years ago, when our production had grown substantially, I realized that we would have to save money if we were ever going to have our own punch press. So, at our Friday morning Bible study, our employees included a prayer asking the Lord for a punch press. One day, when I was visiting one of our vendors in Los Angeles, I realized that he had a punch press that was not being used, standing in the corner of the building. I told him I was looking for a punch press. This one was a 32-ton press, perfect for what we needed. I asked him, "Is that something you would be willing to sell me?"

"Yes. I can sell it to you," he said.

I calmly replied, "How much do you want for it?" I was combing my beard with my hand.

He thought for a few seconds, rubbed his hand under his chin, and said, "You can have it for $15,000."

I looked at the press, then looked at him, and even though I was jumping with excitement on the inside, I said to him in a very cool and calm voice, "I will get back to you."

When I came back to our company, I told the employees what I had found, and we started praying that we could get it at a cheaper price. The next time I went to visit the vendor, I offered him a hammer mill that I had built, which had cost me $200 in scrap metal. Of course, I didn't tell him that. I asked him, "Would you consider trading me your punch press for this hammer mill?"

"You drive a hard bargain, Sören. But because it is you, I can do that," he said.

He must have been in a very good mood because on top of trading me his punch press for my hammer mill, he agreed to deliver the punch press and to send one man to teach me how to operate it. If that isn't a great answer to prayer, I don't know what is.

I told you I would share two more answers to prayer that I received. Here's the second one. We needed a stamping machine, and I had been looking for one on the internet. They cost around the same price as a used punch press: $15,000. One day, I was in San Francisco, visiting one of our distributors, who was located in an old warehouse. Part of the building looked like a barn where they made brooms and mops for cleaning floors. Another part of the building was dark and kind of dirty. While I was walking around the warehouse with the owner, I spotted something in a dark section of the big room. I had the feeling that it was a stamping machine, so I asked the owner, "What is that you have in that corner over there?"

He said, "I don't know what's there. That machine has been standing there ever since we purchased the building."

I took a closer look at it and said, "I think it is a stamping machine." To my surprise, when we dusted it off, I realized it was a 2-ton stamping machine — exactly what we had been praying for.

The owner said, "I never knew what it was, and since we don't have any use for it, you can have it!"

When I brought the stamping machine home, underneath the stamping table, there were two drawers full of dies, which had been used to stamp brooms. When I showed the employees the stamping machine God had given us, I said, "Thank you for your prayers. I didn't even have to bargain for it! One more prayer answered."

2006: My Second Motorcycle

Showing off my Eliminator, bucket stand, and Big Dog chopper.

A poster for my concerts when I toured as a singer. This is available for purchase in my online art gallery.

I still had my Harley-Davidson Road King with 22-inch ape hangers, but I wanted to buy another chopper. On many occasions, I visited a Big Dog motorcycle dealer here in town where they displayed a dozen or so choppers. I fell in love with one of them because it had special artwork that looked like a Dala horse. The Dala horse is a symbol of our state in Sweden. The owner of the company lived in Palm Springs, and the dealership had been using the bike for their television commercials, so it had 100 miles on it. However, it had never been registered yet. I made a deal with the manager. This time, I didn't take the time to ask my wife. The bike cost $45,000, but I knew I could afford it. Many years later, I took that bike back to Sweden and used it in my ministry. You can see this chopper in a commercial if you search for "Big Dog Motorcycles Commercial" on YouTube. You can also see me riding the bike in my video, where I sing "Preacher of the Gospel." Nick Blackwood, a friend of mine from Canada, wrote the song.[1] Then I purchased one more bike for my ministry in the U.S.

2007: Revealing My Biggest Secret

Through the years, I have put on dozens of seminars, teaching the new window cleaning techniques I developed because of my wide-body squeegees. You can watch the videos I've made teaching the Z method, the L method, the upside-down U method, the reverse stroke method, and the multi-squeegee. One of the events I went to was the Gary Mauer summer picnic, 50 miles outside of Milwaukee. This event took place at a ski resort. This summer trip would be very different for me.

When I arrived at the Milwaukee Mitchell International Airport, I went to pick up my rental car, and to my surprise, I found I had forgotten my credit card at home. This was very strange because I had been traveling all over the world, and I had never forgotten the credit card at home. Well,

---

1   https://www.youtube.com/watch?v=mOoPB0SZE4M&list=UULFoggUnL83x2irvsLx
     GV6STA&index=19

no worries; I had cash. The lady at the desk said, "We don't take cash."

Immediately, I got a feeling that God had something up His sleeve. I ended up taking a taxi to the airport hotel, which wasn't too far. I called Gary Mauer and told him what had happened. He suggested that I take a shuttle out to the ski resort the next day, which was Saturday, July 25.

That afternoon, I called the shuttle company and made a reservation for the next morning. The next day, I arrived at the picnic and met many new and old window cleaners. We had a wonderful lunch, and after I did my seminar, I gathered all the Christian window cleaners for a little fellowship. Only a handful of people out of about 60 showed up, but we had an awesome time together. Nancy, from Harry Falk Window Cleaning Supplies Company, was one of the people who joined in.

After the rally, I took the shuttle back to my hotel. Now, I'm going to let you in on the big secret. When I was around 24 years old, the hair on the top of my head, toward the back, started to thin out. So, I went to a hairdresser and shaved the hair off before people could notice it. Then, I had the hairdresser make me a small hairpiece about the size of a tennis ball. The only person who knew about the hairpiece was my Winnie. The hairpiece was of such high quality that I could swim and dive, and it was secure, and, more importantly, no one could tell I had fake hair. Well, over time, the bald spot got bigger and bigger, to the point where my hair was only growing 2 inches above my ears. Although I had some high-quality and very expensive hairpieces that looked natural, I was suspicious that a friend in our church who was a hairdresser, Mrs. Clay from Alaska, knew that I wore a hairpiece. The reason for my suspicion was that every time we had dinner at their home, she always touched my hair and said, "You have such beautiful hair, Sören."

I felt so embarrassed because I thought she was teasing me. She was not the only one who told me I had beautiful hair, so I started to feel embarrassed. I knew the hairpiece was a petroleum-based product, not anything that God had made, and I started to feel fake. At the same time, I had worn my fake hair for so many years, I was scared to death to reveal this to people. I was convinced that I would look pretty stupid without it, but God knew how I felt in my heart about this.

Well, back to the hotel at the Milwaukee Mitchell International Airport. I woke up Sunday morning, and I was ready to go to a local church. I was up early enough to go down and have a continental breakfast. I took a shower, and I went into the room to pick up my hairpiece. But before I had a chance to put it on my head, I heard that voice that I had heard so many years earlier when God had saved my life, and He said, "Sören, you don't need that anymore."

I panicked, and I said, "I can't face my friends without this hairpiece!"

Then He said, "If you have faith in Me, you can do it."

"Yes Lord, I do have faith, but still I don't have the strength to do it."

My head looked like a flat airport because I had fairly long hair on the sides, and my head was rather wide and flat on top, where my bald spot was. I got so stressed out that I started weeping. "I can't do it!"

But I heard Him say, "Trust in the Lord with all your heart."

I said, "I'll try, but I need some confirmation, Lord. I don't think I can do this."

I kept sobbing, and I looked at myself in the mirror, and I looked so stupid. What would people say at my church when I got back to Palm Springs? And what was my wife going to say? Well, I didn't hear any more from the Lord. I felt a little shaken up and amazed to have heard the voice of the Lord again. I didn't feel like going anywhere after this experience, so I stayed in my room. I turned the TV on and started listening to a sermon from some local church. In the middle of the sermon, the pastor said, "You must trust in the Lord with all your heart!"

Right then and there, I knew, 100 percent, that that was the confirmation I needed from God. I don't know how to explain it, but God uses many different ways to talk to us. I started weeping again. I was so touched by hearing the Lord confirm what I had asked for that I went up to the table where my toupee was lying and I took it in my hand.

I said, "I *have* to do it!"

I was looking at the wastepaper basket beside the mirror, but I couldn't let go. I kept sobbing, telling myself I had to drop the hairpiece in the basket. Then I remembered that God said if I had faith in Him, I could do what He asked. I knew I had trusted God up until now. So, I held that hairpiece over the wastepaper basket, and finally, I got the strength to let go of it. Before it even landed in the basket, this overwhelming feeling came over me! I felt the same way as I had when I was born again, and I started laughing, and laughing, and laughing!

I said, "Thank you, Lord! I feel so relieved that I don't have to carry this fake petroleum-made piece anymore!"

After drying my eyes and my face, I looked at myself in the mirror and I said, "You sure look stupid."

Then I got a great idea! I decided to shave my head! I took my electric shaver and started to shave one side. When I was almost done, I was going to start on the other side when, to my surprise, the red light on the shaver turned on. When I went to grab the charger, I realized I had left it back home. I had to go down to the lobby and ask them for a pair of scissors. When I'd arrived at the hotel, I'd had a full head of beautiful wavy hair, and now I was going to take the elevator down to the lobby with a flat head and half of my hair shaved off. I looked like I had put on a swimming cap sideways. This was insane, but I didn't care anymore. My fear was totally gone. I went out into the hallway, pushed the button for the elevator, and when it opened, two people were standing, staring at me! I can't imagine what they were thinking, looking at my weird hairstyle. But they didn't say anything. My biggest surprise was when I came down to the lobby with a totally new look, asking the person at the front desk for a pair of scissors. She looked at me like I was from a different planet! I asked if she had any scissors I could borrow, and she said, "Yes, I think we have a pair in the back."

When she handed them to me, she asked, "Is that all, Mr. Samuelsson?"

I said, "Yes, thank you very much. I will bring them back when I leave for the airport."

I went back up to my room, and again, there were people in the elevator. But I didn't even feel embarrassed anymore. I went up to my room and started to cut the rest of the hair that was left off. Then, I used what was left of the battery in my shaver and shaved off the rest.

What I have to say is that I became a different person. I felt really good. I ordered some food and ate in my room. That afternoon, I took the elevator down to the lobby and returned the scissors and the key. The way they looked at me, they were probably 100 percent sure I was an undercover agent. It was funny. I took the taxi back to the airport. Flying back to Palm Springs, I felt such relief. Now, I understand why God let me forget my credit card at home. He wanted me to stay in that room and listen to him.

After the six-hour flight, I arrived at the Palm Springs International Airport, where Winnie was supposed to pick me up at the curb outside the baggage area. I was wondering what she would say when she saw me completely bald for the first time. All of a sudden, I spotted her coming in her car, and I moved forward so she would see me. But she didn't stop! She just kept driving right past me, even though I was waving my hand. She didn't recognize me! Now I know that she is not looking at other men. She drove around the parking lot once more since she hadn't seen me. After a few minutes she came by a second time, looking for me. This time, I was not going to let her pass by. So I jumped out into the middle of the driveway and waved my hands. I'd never seen my wife's face grow so long! Her jaw dropped like never before! I was kind of worried about what she would say. She stopped and jumped out of the car, and looked at me in shock.

"What did you do? I didn't recognize you!"

And I said to her, "God spoke to me about my hairpiece! He told me I did not need it anymore!"

Winnie said, "You look different, but you're still handsome," and we hugged.

I said, "Thank you, honey."

On Sunday, we went to church, and people didn't even recognize me. They couldn't believe how different I looked without hair. Some of our friends heard rumors there was a new guy in church.

One of the benefits of shaving my head became clear to me when I started to ride my motorcycles. My head felt so much better. Before, when I had worn the helmet, especially when it was around 115 degrees, my hair would start to get very itchy, and sweat would start running down my face. Now that I had no hair, the problem disappeared. So, getting rid of my hairpiece also improved my biker life. Praise the Lord!

2007: Ministering at the American Heat Biker Event in Palm Springs

Cycle event shows spiritual side

American Heat wraps up 3 days; no major arrests

By Sherry Barkas
The Desert Sun

PALM SPRINGS — The thunderous roar of motorcycles grew quiet for about an hour Sunday morning as bikers attended a spiritual service as part of the American Heat event.

About 60 people, many wearing leather vests with the association's logo and "Riding for the Son" motto on the back, listened as Soren Samuelsson, president of the Palm Springs Chapter of the Christian Motorcyclists Association, and others shared their messages of faith and battles with addiction.

The 9 a.m. service kicked off the final day of the three-day event, which police said went off without a major incident.

The only arrests police had made as of Sunday evening were of two men who were suspected of driving their motorcycles under the influence of alcohol on Friday night.

Sgt. Mike Kovaleff didn't have specific details of the arrests.

There was a report of members of the Mongols, motorcycle gang keeping people from a parking lot near Zelda's around 11 p.m. Saturday, but the incident was resolved before police arrived on scene, Palm Springs police Sgt. Gus Araiza said.

Jacinto Mountains as a backdrop Sunday morning, Samuelson took the stage on Palm Canyon Drive at Arenas Road to open a spiritual service by singing "I Pledge Allegiance to the Lamb."

ing 38 years of alcohol abuse, he said.

"I understand people who say they can't quit, because I couldn't quit," he said, describing himself as a workaholic and an alcoholic.

blink of an eye and my life was changed," Samuelson said.

Chaplain for the local chapter of the Christian Motorcyclists Association Virgil Castleberry of Palm Desert said that after years of abuse

quit the drugs and alcohol that had taken center stage in their lives. That was 18 years ago and they have been clean and sober since, he said.

Soren Samuelsson (center), president of the Palm Springs chapter of the Christian Motorcycle Association, is joined by association member Earl Cruikshank of Desert Hot Springs (left) and chapter Chaplin Virgil Castleberry during a Sunday morning spiritual service Sunday on Palm Canyon Drive as part of the American Heat 2011 weekend events. SHERRY BARKAS/THE DESERT SUN

Newspaper clipping of one of my events, American Heat 2011, in Palm Springs.

I have been going to the American Heat biker event ever since that day so many years ago when I left the church Bible Study. By attending this great event, I got to know a very nice couple, Richard and Jenny Hardesty of J C and Us Ministries from Bakersfield. They also promoted the Boss Hos motorcycle with a 502 V8, which I got to take for a ride when they first came out. Richard was in charge of the Sunday morning service at the American Heat event for many years, and for several of those years, he had asked me to come up and preach and sing some songs. In 2006, he asked me if I could do the Sunday morning service because he had broken his leg, and he also had some other appointments.

I said, "Thank you very much! I never expected to be asked to do something like this!"

Just to be sure, I called the organizer for Roadshow to confirm with them that they would let me do it. But they had known me through the years when I worked with Richard. So, on October 7, 2007, I led my first Sunday morning biker service. This was a very exciting time in my life! Roadshow were the organizers for the whole event, and they had a big stage in downtown Palm Springs on the main street in front of a Starbucks coffee shop. I rented 100 chairs and also some pop-up tents. In the past, people who attended the service had stood outside in the sun, and I did not want to put them through that ordeal. The crowd grew every year, and I had the opportunity to preach the gospel and sing Christian songs in front of a whole bunch of rough-looking bikers. I didn't look that friendly myself, and that might be the reason so many bikers came to listen to me. The head of the event noticed that we were able to get more people to come than in previous years, so they asked me to continue doing it the following year.

I had a talk with my friend Richard, who had gotten me in there to begin with. I told him about the success we had had and that the event organizer asked me if I would be willing to lead the services the following year.

Richard said, "You go ahead and lead the ministry there next year. I've got other places to preach."

Well, this new ministry was something that would continue for a few years. I did my best, not realizing that God was preparing me for the next project He had planned for me. God allowed me to grow and learn in this biker's ministry because He was getting me ready to start a similar ministry across the globe in Sweden, my homeland.

In 2008, the Lord spoke to me again. He said, "Sören, go to Sweden, to Liljekvistska Park, and preach the gospel for seven years." The park is located in the middle of town. Here, they have a big stage and events like the one in Palm Springs, in my hometown. For seven years?

I said, "Lord, I can't do that. Just thinking about it makes me nervous. The people back home — they still remember me. I don't have enough faith to do this."

I told Winnie what God had asked me to do, and she said, "It is up to you."

In the meantime, I continued to lead the Palm Springs event and serve in the prison ministry. I had the opportunity to be used by the Holy Spirit to lead dozens of inmates to Christ. I was also starting to be invited to sing in different churches. I set up events in different cities where I would share my testimonies, sing my songs, and read the Scriptures. Wherever I went, I had a bunch of bikers with me. Most of them were members of the CMA and a local group, the Sword of the Lord biker ministry. I would ask many of them to share their testimonies so people could hear about how Jesus Christ had saved them and changed their lives. We were around 20 Harley bikers: Daniel, Virgil, Earl, Pastor Wes, and many more, and believe me, none of them looked like your typical Christian. But you knew they were the moment you began to talk to them. I was still involved in our company, but from 2001 to 2009, I was very much involved in the biker ministry.

2009: Riding to Chama, New Mexico, with the CMA

Advertisement for one of my concerts after winning
first place in a 2009 talent contest.

I was still the president of our chapter in Palm Desert. So, the chaplain in our chapter decided we should take a ride to Chama, New Mexico, to attend a large CMA rally. When we got to the rally, we learned there was a talent contest for any bikers who wanted to participate. I signed up to sing "Riding for Him." This was a song my friend from Canada, Nick Blackwood, had written. Well, wouldn't you know it! I took the first place with that song! As I mentioned, Nick Blackwood also wrote "Preacher of the Gospel." You can watch the video on YouTube if you search for Swede Samuelsson.

As I mentioned previously in this book, I have a few songs that I recorded, which you can hear on YouTube. If you go to "Bill Glass Fresno May 4 5 2012," you can watch Mark Flower use my song in that video. Through the years, Joe Manley and I did ministry work in downtown Palm Springs every Thursday. We witnessed to people while handing out tracts from our CMA chapter. Those nights, I handed out my music CDs to people. One person who got one of my Christmas CDs later surprised me by putting a YouTube video together in which I sing "Mary, Did You Know?" He sure did a good job.

2009: Launching the Ultra-Light Squeegee Channel

My daughter modeling Sörbo products.

In 2009, we developed our fifth squeegee model. This ultra-light squeegee channel was made in sizes ranging from 6 inches to 18 inches only. We used the channel that we had developed for the Tricket, the handheld squeegee tong I invented in 1973 for cleaning louvered windows. But besides the wide-body squeegee that I invented, I wanted to develop the lightest squeegee on the market, and that had to be a standard channel. This was made of very high-grade aircraft aluminum. I wanted it to be the standard for high-grade aluminum squeegees in the industry. This was also to be the lightest squeegee on the market because it was developed to be part of the ultra-light squeegee line. We developed our ultra-light squeegee to be very streamlined for easy maneuverability. We would be entering this high-performance squeegee in the world competition for speed cleaning. This event is held at the IWCA convention every year. This superlight squeegee handle was designed without the rubber grip on our 12-inch ultra-light squeegee to make it as light as possible. To this day, our squeegee is the lightest competition squeegee in the world, and it is still the lightest, most rigid squeegee on the market. Our 18-inch model, completely assembled, weighs only 2.5 ounces. The channel was made to also fit the standard squeegee blades with the round back. Our new model was recognized by the window cleaning industry almost immediately as the lightest squeegee ever sold on the market.

2009: Mission Trip to the Philippines

During this time, I introduced the CMA ministry in Sweden and started a chapter there. Winnie had a strong feeling that God wanted her to go back home to the Philippines to help the people who lived up in the mountain regions. She had a vision to build a school where children in the village could learn how to read the Bible. Every year, for seven years, Winnie directed the construction and opening of a new school in a new village. We had dozens of little kids attending our kindergarten schools in those villages. Winnie was doing miraculous work!

In 2009, I felt like I wanted to join her and preach the gospel to the inhabitants. So, Winnie, our daughter Mindi, our good friend Cheryl Sherwood from our church, Winnie's brother who lived there, and I made preparations so I could preach the gospel and help minister to the needs of the villagers. We were all so excited!

The day finally came to leave on our mission trip. We flew to Manila, but as I got out of the plane, I pinched a nerve in my lower back! The pain was so bad I instantly fell to the ground. I felt like I had been struck by a bolt of lightning. Once on the ground, I could not get up on my own. I had to be lifted off the ground and placed in a wheelchair. I had to travel in that wheelchair in between flights all the way to Davao City, where they picked us up to take us to the village. I was lifted off the wheelchair and placed in a small Jeep, which got us to our final destination.

I was a little bit upset because I knew that the dark spirits did not want me to preach the gospel to the villagers in the Philippines. However, when we arrived, all my friends and family who were believers laid hands on me and prayed for complete healing. I told myself I would not get upset if I had to stay in bed while I was there. I told everyone, "I will pray for you guys."

I really didn't think that I would be of much use during this mission trip after this incident. I knew from previous incidents like this that sometimes it took at least a week to recover, and this is the very reason I had invented the high bucket stand. But to my joyful amazement, the next morning, I woke up and felt completely well! I had been healed! I felt fine, and I had no pain! My physical strength was totally restored! I was miraculously healed, and now I was ready to start to do our ministry work!

The following Saturday, my brother-in-law invited around 25 people from different Indigenous groups to come to the village to hear the gospel of Jesus Christ. I had already arranged for one of our schoolteachers to be the translator. That afternoon I met a lot of different people dressed in their wonderful and colorful traditional garments. In the afternoon, we started the service. I explained where I came from and how God had transformed my life. I read the Scriptures and worshiped God with some singing. Finally, I ended the service by inviting anyone who wanted to become a Christian to approach the altar for prayer. To my great surprise, 25 of the people attending decided to live for the Lord Jesus! What a blessing! The next day, the ladies went into the village and invited the wives to come to a Bible meeting, where they actually led five more ladies to Christ.

Our mission work in the Philippines has helped my faith to grow. Through the years, we have helped the people in the villages where we have established schools by providing education, food, clothing, and even healthcare for the children who were born with facial defects such as cleft palate. We have paid for their operations through the financial growth and prosperity of our company. I will never forget the first mission trip I went on to help my wife Winnie establish schools in those villages. Although I don't go anymore, Winnie is still operating this ministry, and Sörbo Products and the ministry partners provide everything those little children need to learn to read, to be fed, to be clothed, to be healthy, and to learn about Jesus Christ.

2010: Introducing Jam-Proof End Tips for Extension Poles

For many years, the window cleaning industry had a problem with the end tips getting jammed on the squeegee handles attached to extension poles. Sometimes the problem was so bad that you actually had to stand on the T-bar to separate the squeegee handle from the extension pole. The solution to this problem was not mine. It was given to me by a professional window cleaner I met at one of the trade shows I attended. We were having a discussion about the problem of extension pole end tips that got jammed inside squeegee handles. He suggested the idea of using an O-ring on the extension pole end tip. This would give the squeegee handle the ability to slide off the extension pole end tip if enough pressure was used to pull the two pieces of equipment apart. The O-ring would also provide enough friction to keep the squeegee handle on the extension pole during use. It was like adding wheels with brakes on a car.

When I came back home, I tested the idea. I made an extension pole end tip that had three high-quality rubber O-rings on the end, and to my pleasant surprise, the idea worked! The reason I used a total of three O-rings was so that a window cleaner could use up to three O-rings to achieve the right friction necessary for his extension pole and squeegee handle. It was really effective because it kept the squeegee handle firmly on the end tip, but at the same time, the extension pole did not jam up inside the squeegee handle. When you pulled it off, it slid off very slowly, with just the right friction, and the same thing happened when you put it on. By putting the handle on with less force, the rubber O-rings would firmly grab the handle and keep it secured. And if you wanted to reduce the friction even more, you could remove one or two of the O-rings. This actually eliminated the problem of jammed-up squeegee handles on extension poles. I named it the Sörbo Jam-Proof End Tip. By increasing the outside dimension of the little ribs that go into the tubing, I designed the new Jam-Proof End Tip so it would not be loose and rattle on the extension pole. When you put it on the pole the first time, the tubing will shave the excess plastic off. However, this creates the perfect tight fit. You might need to use a hammer to get it on the first time, but you get a very good connection all the way from your hand grip to the window.

I believe that in 2011, the other companies started to make new end tips because of this very same problem. They made their end tips with the fast-release button to keep the handle from falling off. But this did not take care of the second problem; the squeegee handle still rattled when you attached it to the pole. This is why we have the most secure end tip on the market today. It is the most solid pole on the market, and a real professional window cleaner understands the benefits of this invention.

In 2010, I was recognized by the Window Cleaning Hall of Fame.

Singing in front of the Christian Motorcycle
Association at their 2010 convention.

2011: Ready to Start New Ministry in Sweden

Newspaper clipping from Sweden while I was touring
and spreading the gospel on a motorbike.

Clipping continued ...

Clipping continued ...

In 2011, all of a sudden, this feeling came over me to go to Sweden and start the ministry. It had been two years since the Lord had spoken to me about starting a ministry in Sweden, and now, He had increased my faith enough to do so. I immediately said to Winnie, "Do you remember when the Lord spoke to me and told me to go to Sweden?"

Winnie said, "Yes, I remember."

"Well honey, I'm ready to go!"

So she said, "Go!"

I started to prepare everything for my new ministry. First, we needed a place to stay, so I started looking on the internet for an old house to purchase. I spotted one built in 1890, which kept speaking to me. It was fully furnished and ready for us to move in. I said to Winnie, "I wonder if God wants us to have that house?"

I looked at exchange rates for the dollar to the Swedish crown, and after praying for a while, I realized the value of the dollar had started to go down, and I said, "Maybe this is a sign that this house wasn't meant for us."

Three months later, I started looking at the value of the dollar again, and it had gone up. "Well, that house must be sold by now," said Winnie.

But when I looked, it was still on the market. I told Winnie, "Maybe God wants us to have that house anyway, honey."

So I called the real estate office in Sweden and asked them about the house, and they said many people had been looking at it, but it was still available. Then, the real estate agent said they were going to have an open house that Wednesday. This was starting to get exciting! I called my brother, Leif, who didn't live very far from where the house was located and asked him to go and look at it. The real estate lady told my brother there was a lady coming to look at the house also. So, I started praying that the lady would not come. When he called me the next day, my brother told me it was a really nice house, built in 1890 and fully furnished. He said it would be a good buy.

"What happened to the other lady?" I asked.

My brother said, "She never came."

Right away, I purchased the house. The next week, when I saw the house with my own eyes, I knew that God was behind the whole thing. The house was furnished with everything — even a little wooden box with sewing needles and threads — all the dishes, drinking glasses, coffee cups, and all kinds of other dishes. It was amazing! The upstairs section of the house was full of antique items. We all went down to the real estate office, and I was introduced to the owner. I found out that the wife had inherited this home from her family, going back all the way to 1890. They had only used it a couple of weeks every year during the summer while their kids were growing up. But now that the kids were all grown up, the owners didn't spend anymore time there except to mow the lawn and to do maintenance work on it. They had two other homes. The owners gave me two photos of the couple who had built the house, which showed them sitting on the front porch. Later on, we found a basket full of letters that they had received from relatives who had moved to America in the 1800s. It was really cool.

The house was built on an acre of land with the forest right behind it. There was a big field below where there were a couple of horses. I asked the real estate lady who the horses belonged to. She didn't know, but she had heard that somebody was going to build a new home there. I said that would be a disaster because this neighborhood real estate was from the old days. I did not think it would be a good thing to put a new home in the middle of it. So I started praying immediately that we would find the owner and buy this property, and keep it the way it was. When we found out who it was, I contacted the owner and told him what I was thinking and that I wanted to buy the land from him. He told me it was their son's friend who wanted to build on it, but they had not purchased the property yet. We started praying again that God would change their mind, and after a week, the owner called me and told me I could buy it. I knew that they had increased the price because I was very interested in buying the land, but I didn't mind that at all. We finally got the deed, and that field is still full of wildflowers every spring. After we purchased the house, I purchased a sound system, and I was ready for the next summer when I would start doing my seven years of ministry work in downtown Borlänge in the park.

2012: Going to Los Angeles Prison

Ever since I became a Christian, I've been a member of the largest Christian motorcycle group in the world, the Christian Motorcycle Association, also known as the CMA. As a result of joining the CMA, I became a part of Bill Glass Ministries. In 2012, we visited the prisons in Los Angeles and Fresno. My time and experience during those years doing prison ministry was awesome! It was during that time that I also met the founder of the Big Outlaw Biker Organization. He, like me, had been saved in the later days of his life. That year would be the year I went on what would become a wild experience in the Los Angeles prison. The CMA is made up of over 180,000 Christian motorcyclist members from all over the world. I had the privilege of serving as the president of our local chapter in Palm Desert for six years.

One weekend in May of 2012, a bunch of bikers and I rode to the Los Angeles prison to show off our bikes and minister to the inmates. We spent a full day in the prison yard with 200 inmates. Some of us preferred to go into the lockups. Every time we go to prisons, we have been blessed to lead many inmates to Christ. On that occasion, in the afternoon, the time came for us to show off our "burnouts" on our choppers and motorcycles.

We usually performed our burnout stunts on asphalt, but in this case, we were going to do it on a very smooth basketball court, which was basically a cement slab. This meant that the level of friction working against our back tires would be very different from what we were accustomed to. We actually had a couple of guys who almost laid their bikes down — a very scary experience (when riders are faced with imminent danger or realize that an accident is inevitable, they tend to lay down their bikes to lessen the effects of the accident), and they ended up quitting.

When my turn came up, I did not back down from the challenge. I was riding my 117 cc Big Dog K9 chopper with the 300 tire in the back. The cement slab was surrounded by bleachers where 200 inmates were standing and sitting, watching with great excitement. As I approached the court for my turn, I noticed that about 80 feet in front of me, there was a small 8-foot opening between the bleachers. That was the tiny "eye of the needle" that I was going to have to pass through if I was going to survive the stunt. I realized that by the time I reached the small exit, I would be traveling up to 50 miles an hour. On the other side of the bleachers was a baseball field, and in the corner was the pit area, surrounded by three steel posts with steel netting. I figured the distance was long enough to give me a chance to turn before I reached the dead-end zone. So, with 120 horses of torque on my back wheel, I started my burnout, aiming at the small opening flanked by the cheering inmates on each side. I could tell they were excited to see me perform my burnout while I drove by at a very high speed. Winding up the engine to 3,000 RPM, I let the clutch out, and my bike took off, burning the tires. I increased the RPMs to their max capacity, then I instantly slammed the second gear. The metal beast on wheels roared, then jerked and suddenly changed direction, taking me off course. Instantly, I realized that I was on a direct course to slam into the bleachers. My instincts as a motorcycle driver took over. I didn't let off the throttle. Instead, I tried my best to steer my speeding chopper so that I would not hit the bleachers. I came so close to the bleachers that I scraped my leg on the metal. Miraculously, I went flying by the inmates at blazing speed. When I came out the other side, the bleachers went up in a loud cheer! Afterward, my fellow CMA members said I had almost ripped the shirt off one of the inmates who was standing at the edge of the bleachers.

I was so relieved to have survived the first part of the stunt that I didn't have enough time to concentrate on what was facing me beyond the bleachers. I came out onto the dirt field at such a high speed, I realized now that I was going to crash straight into those steel posts. I knew braking wouldn't do any good on the loose dirt, especially with that narrow tire in the front and the 300 tire in the back. The tires were designed for riding on hard surfaces, not on clay fields. The only option I had was to lay the speeding bike down myself. So, I stepped on the brake and threw myself down on my left side on the ground. Because I didn't have a helmet on, my head hit the ground extremely hard ... and I fainted. I was only unconscious for an instant. When I came to, I was still traveling to my doom at high speed, sliding flat on the ground, still sitting on the bike with my left leg trapped underneath it. I could see the steel posts coming closer and closer, and it looked like my face and the post were going to meet head-on. I cried, "Lord, help me!" I tried to sink my head in between my shoulders as much as I could before the impact.

I must have blacked out. I woke up hearing my biker friends screaming, "Hey Swede, how are you doing?"

"I am fine!" I exclaimed in relief.

I was still sitting on the bike, lying flat on the ground on my left side. My leg was still underneath the bike. I didn't feel anything. Blood was running down my face, and I realized I had skinned the top of my bald head on the post. I think that is why I passed out. The CMA guys lifted the bike off my body and helped me up. Thank God I hadn't broken my left leg again. This was the leg I had twisted under my Road King six months earlier. I'd had to have surgery to install a metal rod in my leg. That is probably what had prevented my leg from breaking again.

Well, the bikers helped me up to the security desk, and they told me that they had to call the ambulance. I told officers, "If you call an ambulance, you have to pay for it. I am fine. I just have to rest a little bit and then I'll probably go home."

So, I got some ice cubes for my leg, and after 45 minutes, I decided to look at the bike. As expected, there was quite a bit of damage. The headlight was hanging to the side, the footpeg was broken, and the license plate, which was on the side of the bike, was also broken. I asked the guard if they had any duct tape, and he brought me a whole roll. The funny thing is that the duct tape was the same color as the bike: orange! I taped everything up and then I took off and drove back down to the desert.

Two days later, the swelling had not gone down. I went to the doctor, and he emptied the blood in my leg, which looked like a balloon. But I later heard from my biker friends that the inmates said it was the best show they had ever seen in the Los Angeles prison. My friends told me, as soon as I had laid my bike down, all they had seen was a big dust cloud, so they hadn't really seen how close I had come to smashing my face into that steel post. After a couple of weeks, we took a ride up to Fern Valley, where the Christian bikers had a big event, with barbecues and fellowshipping. When the biker who had arranged this event was up on the stage speaking, he saw me, and he said, "Here is the Swede! The only biker who ever crashed his bike in Los Angeles prison!" The incident that day had obviously been a big hit.

2012: My First Concert in Sweden, Saturday, July 28, 2012

I made a very nice ad for the two biggest newspapers in town with a photo of myself on my chopper. The headline was "Good News on Two Wheels: Christian biker from California is here to tell you about Jesus!"

I didn't really know if even one person would show up. I had arranged to use the stage in downtown Borlänge, which was my old hometown. I personally never knew any people who were Christians when I lived there. I didn't really know what was going to happen. But God told me everything would be fine. When Saturday came, and I started my first concert, 60 people were in front of me, listening to me speaking and singing. Among them was a large number of my old friends. I believe they came to see if I had lost my mind. But because of my singing and the Holy Spirit helping me to read the Scriptures, it turned out to be a very blessed event. I told them that Jesus had told me to do this every year for seven years. To my surprise, many of them told me they would be back the following year. They were surprised that I was singing and that I was a believer in Christ. This became a yearly event, and I thank the Lord for arranging everything.

Our ministry grew when we started to spend the summers over there, and we were blessed with some wonderful neighbors. During the years of this ministry, I was invited to speak and sing in many churches in Scandinavia. I ministered in Sweden, Finland, Norway, and Denmark, and many came to Christ. I was also interviewed on radio stations; God really blessed my socks off, like they say!

2013: Introducing the Aluminum Fast-release Handle

In 2013, we released an aluminum squeegee handle. In the past, we had marketed all the Sörbo squeegee models with the patented fast-release swivel handle by changing the lower jaw — now made of stainless steel — to fit this superlight aluminum handle. We made the lever in three different colors to designate to which squeegee each belongs. The black lever fits the 90-degree Black Mamba, and the 45-degree VIPER 45, which was developed a few years later. The purple lever fits the Cobra, the Q-Cobra, and the Silverado. The yellow lever fits the Ultralight and the Ultra 45-degree channel. At the shows, window cleaners were surprised at how light and rigid the ultralight squeegee was, and it became very popular. This particular squeegee was also designed for the standard round squeegee rubbers and, of course, our T-shaped squeegee rubber that I had invented in 1985. It's universal, so it fits all the squeegee channels on the market.

2014: Avenal State Prison, Kings County, California

I have to tell you about another biker miracle. During the years visiting the state prisons in the surrounding counties in Fresno, we experienced many miracles. But this one is really cool. It was a Friday afternoon, and we were riding back to our hotel in Fresno. We were 15 bikers riding staggered. I was the second biker in line, and Virgil Castleberry, our chaplain, was riding behind me. We had been riding for about 30 minutes, and at one of the red lights, the last biker in line was riding a trike. He came up beside me, and he asked me who Virgil was.

"He is our chaplain," I said.

"I've got his prison pass, and you won't believe how I got it! I'll tell you at the next gas station," he said, with a huge grin on his face.

When we stopped at the gas station to fill up and use the men's room, the guy explained what had happened. He told us he was the last in our line of bikers. There were thirteen bikers between himself and Virgil, our chaplain. All of a sudden, he saw something like a piece of paper fly up in the air at the front of the line, and it started to swirl around. We were riding around 55 miles an hour on a narrow road out in the farmland, and all of a sudden, when it came closer to him, it landed on his lip, and he grabbed it. It was then that he realized it was the prison pass for the next day. He knew it was very important to give it back to the owner, or he wouldn't get in the next day. We have seen other things like this happen, and we simply realize that because we are soldiers for Jesus doing something that many Christians don't want to do, God shows up in different ways; yes, to let us know that He is around. As some of you know already, God has a sense of humor.

2015: Introducing the California Dream Pole

Modeling our new toolbelt and the California Dream Pole.

For many years, I had dreamed about developing a custom-design extension pole. I wanted to make it of aluminum for one reason: we'd never had one on the market. I wanted to make one that would stay locked with a short twist of the handle. I also wanted to make one that didn't take in water and dirt when cleaning windows. I wanted it to have a very thin twist lock; something you couldn't do with plastic parts because they were too bulky. So, in 2015, I designed the first aircraft aluminum locking device that would clamp on the inner tubing like a pit bull. I named it the California Dream Pole because it was a dream come true.

I am a very patriotic person, so everything I have invented was made in the U.S. I designed a new type of nylon friction shim inside the pole, which can be replaced. I also designed a nylon dust protection shim that protects the inner tubing and prevents dirt and water from getting into the interior of the aluminum lock. Both of these nylon shims are replaceable and can be ordered at our dealers. We also added a rubber grip right below the twist lock for a slip-free grip when your hands are wet. This is a high-performance pole and, therefore, requires a little bit of maintenance. We recommend that the operator unscrew the collar and lubricate it with waterproof grease every six months because it is anodized aluminum, and it needs some type of lubrication when it has been used for a long time. Please look at the "California Dream EXTENSION POLE by Sorbo" video on YouTube for instructions on how to service this new high-tech pole. The pole is made in two sizes: a 4- to 8-foot design for storefronts and residential window cleaning, and a smaller version that is 1.5 to 3 feet, specially designed with high-rise window cleaning in mind. You can use it for squeegeeing with one hand, and remember to use our popular fast-release handle with a special outlet for the safety line on top of the upper jaw so you can still use this extension pole in a safe way.

2016: Radio Interview in Djurås

During my seven years of ministry in Sweden, I did a few radio interviews about my event, Good News on Two Wheels. Anders, at the radio station Radio Dala in the municipality of Gagnef, in Djurås, asked me if I could come back and speak on the radio on Friday, July 21, 2016 — the day before my concert in Borlänge. I arrived there in the morning, and Anders told me that there was another very well-known evangelist coming, too. His name was Målle.

"Are you kidding? Wow! Then I am going to ask him for forgiveness!" I exclaimed.

"What do you mean?" asked Anders.

I told him we had thrown eggs and tomatoes at him in Borlänge, 57 years earlier. Anders said, "Oh please don't tell him that, especially when he is here! He's going to get really upset!"

"I have to!" I said. "That was one of the first really bad things I did as a kid."

A few minutes later, Målle showed up, looking really sharp for his age. He looked like Buffalo Bill with his long blond hair. He was accompanied by two other men who looked like bodyguards. After talking a bit with Målle, Anders introduced me. I told him how great it was to finally meet him again and that I had been a Christian since 1999. I told him that the first thing I did after getting saved was to go to Sweden and ask a few people for forgiveness and that now I would like to ask him for forgiveness.

He said, "What do you mean?"

I said, "Do you remember fifty-seven years ago you traveled from city to city, and you were followed by the newspapers wherever you went? Being in Sweden, you were ridiculed for talking about Jesus. As a Christian, it was like being in Sodom and Gomorrah, I imagine. I know that wherever you went, people threw eggs and tomatoes at you, and it became a trend. When you came to my hometown, Borlänge, there were a dozen crazy guys and myself who decided to continue the tradition. So we purchased a couple of cartons of eggs and tomatoes, and I remember so well when you came out on the stage that it didn't take long before the crowd started to load up on you. The eggs and tomatoes started to fly and you got one raw egg right in your forehead. That's when the organizer dragged you off the stage. On behalf of all my friends and myself, I want to ask you for forgiveness."

Målle looked at me and said, "Get down on your knees and ask for forgiveness."

I went down on my knees on the floor in front of him, and I clamped my hands together above my head and said, "Please forgive me, Målle, for what we did to you in Borlänge."

All of a sudden, everybody started laughing, and Målle said, "Get up! You're forgiven!" We were laughing our heads off! After that, we had a good time joking around, and we ended up trading CDs.

Every year for many years, there was a big revival event way in the forest, in the little place called Lovsjön, where Målle was preaching the whole week, and he invited me to come and sing and speak the next day, which was a Saturday. I said, "I am honored that you asked me. I would love to do that, but I have my own event, Good News on Two Wheels, in Borlänge tomorrow."

After the interviews, I left, and it was the last time I saw him. It was a blessing to be able to have met this legend. On top of that, in 2019, a Christian promoter, Bengt Nordström, invited me to sing at his Christian Country and Western event in Boulognerskogen, Gävle, which is on the east coast of Sweden. I met many Christian artists, and many of them I have met again through the years during my ministry.

After the event, we went out for dinner at our hotel, and one of the entertainers told me that he had been working with Målle when he was traveling around the country. I told him about the incident when I asked Målle for forgiveness at the radio station, Radio Dala, in the municipality of Gagnef, in Djurås, so many years earlier. To my surprise, he was one of the bodyguards who had been there at the radio station. It's amazing how God brings people together. The next day, I was invited to speak and sing in a church in Gävle, and the pastor wanted me to tell that story, so I did. The people in the church thought it was a really good testimony.

2016: Surrounded by a Circle of Raindrops

One summer, when I did my ministry in Sweden, Winnie asked me to take her to the local mall, called Kupolen, in Borlänge. When we got there, I told her I would wait outside. I took a seat on the bench. That day, there was a totally blue sky — not a single cloud — so I thought I would sit down and enjoy the beautiful weather. There was a man sitting on the opposite end of the bench, and I found out, after talking to him, that he was also waiting for his wife, who was shopping. I struck up a conversation with him, and after talking for a while, I asked him, "Do you mind if I ask you a personal question?" This is what I asked people all the time, and most of them looked a little surprised.

"Well," he said, "I guess it's okay."

"Do you know where you go when you die?" I asked.

"What do you mean?" he asked me, with a little confusion on his face. Most people feel that way when I ask them the question.

Then, I repeated the same question. "Do you know where you go when you die?"

He looked at me a little confused and said, "Well, some people say, to heaven, I think. Some say six feet under. And some say they don't know."

"Well, you obviously don't know where you're going," I said. "You have to be born again as a Christian, which means that you have a relationship with Jesus. Once you choose to do that, you start your eternal life. You have to decide if you want to be born again. It's a choice you make, and once you do, you ask Jesus into your heart and He will transform you into a new person like He did with me. Not until then will you believe everything in the Bible. That's when you see clearly for the first time. I'll tell you one thing: I did it when I was fifty-five years old, and it is the best decision I ever made."

As soon as I said that, something miraculous happened! Remember, there was a clear blue sky; not a cloud in sight. All of a sudden, large drops of water started to drip down around us, and if you can imagine, there were, like, 2 inches in between these big drops, and they were just about a quarter-inch in diameter. When they landed, they made a dark spot in the cement, and I said, "Look at this!"

We both looked around, and we realized the rain was covering a perfect 20-foot circle around our bench. He said, "Where is it coming from?"

We both looked up at the clear blue sky. There was not one single cloud anywhere, and we were way too far from the mall building for somebody to be pouring water around us from a hose or watering can. I realized God was showing up again, and I said to the man, "This is obviously God showing that He is here with us!"

I felt so blessed to have witnessed another miracle, and all of a sudden, it stopped, but the marks on the cement were still there for anybody who walked by to see. I gave him a couple of tracts, and soon, his wife came back from doing her shopping, and she also looked at that round circle around us, completely covered with these big dark stains from the water drops. She couldn't believe it! I said to them, "Read this tract together when you get home, and then buy a Bible and start reading the Gospel of John because this was truly a sign for you."

2016: From the Jordan River Straight to Heaven

A Swedish friend of mine who also used to be a missionary, Lennart Nyberg, invited me and Winnie to join him on a tour of the Holy Land, Israel. It was a great experience to see all the places that we had been reading about in the Bible. While we were on the tour, a pastor invited us to be baptized in the famous Jordan River. I was so excited to be baptized in the same river as my Savior, Jesus, but I didn't expect it to be so cold. It was New Year's Day, and people were dressed in winter clothes, winter hats, and winter gloves. I remember Winnie asking me, "Are you sure you want to go down in that ice-cold river?"

"Yes! I have to. It might be the only chance I get!"

All those who were going to be baptized that day were dressed in thin white garments that looked like nightgowns. My feet were already freezing cold, and I said, "Lord, I don't know if I can walk down there barefoot."

All of a sudden, I saw a pair of slippers. I stuck my feet in those, and they fit me perfectly. I looked around to see if somebody had left them there to go to the restroom, but after a while, nobody showed up, so I walked down to the Jordan

River, and as soon as I put my toe in the water, I said to myself, *This will probably be my last day on earth.*

Remember, I was coming from Palm Springs, where the temperature is 85 degrees. Well, I had to stand in line for a few minutes, and when I walked into the water, I said to myself, *I'll probably go straight from the Jordan River up to heaven,* because I was sure I would get a heart attack, it was so freezing cold. Finally, I was submerged under the water by the pastor, and when I came up out of the freezing cold water, my nose was more or less blue, and I was shaking like a tail on a rattlesnake. But I actually survived it, and it was a blessing that one of the brothers was videotaping the whole event, so I have a really good memory of my baptism.

After my baptism experience, my wife wanted to do some shopping, so we walked around in the gift shops. Quite a few people who met me in the gift shops told me I looked like Bryan Cranston, the actor who starred in the TV series, *Breaking Bad.* Some teenagers actually asked me if they could take a picture with me. Ever since the show came out on TV, people, from time to time, want to take pictures with me as a look-alike of this movie star. I was not even aware of this show until I went on this trip to the Holy Land.

When I came back to the United States, I actually looked up the show to see if there was some resemblance between Bryan Cranston and me. I guess we're close enough in appearance because people keep asking me if I'm him, and they want to have a picture of me with them. Just recently, I went to the pool store to buy some chemicals for my pool, and a lady in the store said to me, "Hey! You're the *Breaking Bad* guy. My granddaughter is watching it on TV right now! Can I have a picture with you and show her that I met Bryan Cranston? She's really going to get a kick out of it!"

I agreed, so she took the picture to show her granddaughter. That was a truly funny and unexpected experience from a vacation to Israel.

2018: Introducing the First Pivoting Window Scraper on the Market

The Sörbo 6-inch Scraper is the most efficient scraper on the market. One of the benefits is that it requires very little pressure to use effectively. The reason we chose to introduce a pivoting window scraper was that some window cleaners asked me to make a scraper that could tilt back and forth so they could clean the bottom of the windows with an extension pole. I agreed to come up with a new design, and in 2018, we added a pivoting feature to our already-popular scraper. The new scraper became a big seller as it was the first scraper on the market with a pivoting head. Every scraper on the market was fixed at that time. One of the reasons our scraper is so efficient is that we use carbon steel razor blades instead of stainless steel blades. The only setback to using carbon steel blades is that you have to take the razor blade out after each day and dry it; otherwise, it will rust overnight. But the performance is out of this world. The upside to our pivoting scrapers is that no other scraper is able to remove paint, grime, and dirt from any window with only one swipe.

I have even shown videos on YouTube of me fanning a window with this 6-inch scraper like you do with the squeegee. When I finished, the window was totally dry, with not a single streak. And, with the Sörbo Glide in the water, you reduce the friction even more, which is a must to get the best performance out of the scraper. Using our scraper has another benefit: when you scrape your windows before using the squeegees, it reduces the amount of friction and grime that the squeegee must pass over. This prolongs the life of the rubber blade on your squeegees, and it saves you effort, money, and time.

Sörbo's Arm. Patented in 2018 after I purchased the invention from a talented window washer.

Carl Pedersen Lifetime Achievement Award

Sörbo Samuelsson

The IWCA Board of Directors and membership awards you the inaugural Carl Pedersen Lifetime Achievement Award for your outstanding achievements and advancements of the window cleaning industry.

February 9, 2018

2018

My IWCA Lifetime Achievement Award from 2018.

2018: Seven Years of Ministry in Sweden Comes to an End

The seven years that I was told to do ministry in Sweden ended, and there were a couple of years I couldn't go home, but I did the seven years, and it was a tremendous experience. I had learned a lot through the years. I learned that I could do things with the help of the Holy Spirit that I would never have been able to do on my own, and I had the opportunity to lead people to Christ, which were things I never would have dreamed of doing. But I have shown enough proof to many of my old friends how dramatically a person can change, and it was a journey I'll never forget. Thank you, Lord Jesus.

At this time, I was told there was a lot of activity on the internet about my products, so I started looking at YouTube. I also spotted a new company entering the window cleaning industry, duplicating everything that was on the market already. I could see that the industry was growing, so I got inspired to start inventing new products again.

2020: Summer House in Sweden Catches Fire

In May 2020, around 4 p.m., we were sitting in the living room with our daughter and grandchildren when the phone rang. I realized it was my neighbor in Sweden. I answered the phone and said, "How are you doing?"

He said, "I'm doing fine, but I'm sorry to tell you that your house just burned down."

The first thing I said in response was, "So you had a nice Fourth of July fireworks!"

He said, "I am here at your house right now, taking pictures. I will send them to you."

This was around 1:30 a.m. in Sweden. They are nine hours ahead of Pacific time over there. I immediately told my family that our house had burned down, and Winnie started weeping. This was very surprising to all of us. The house was built in 1890 with 12-inch fir tree logs from the forest. It had a lot of history, and it was all original. We lost a lot of antique furniture in the fire that day. Through the years, I had done a lot of work on it, which I had finished the year before.

The next day, my neighbor sent me photos, and I realized that it wasn't as bad as it sounded. The bottom floor was still intact, but the fire crew had sprayed high-pressure water and damaged a lot of furniture. Thank God it was a timber house, made of very old timber, which doesn't burn. It was only charred, and the whole bottom floor was repairable, based on what I could see from the pictures he'd sent. The insurance company said it was a total loss, and they were willing to pay me what they thought the house was worth. Or they said I could rebuild it, but they said it would be better if I tore it down and built a new house. I didn't like that idea.

A week later, when I arrived in Sweden, we started to remove all the burned wood from the house. My neighbor had a tractor and he removed the rest of the stuff on the ground, and we also had some friends who came to help us remove all the water-damaged furniture, which we put into a container. During this time, we were praying that we would find some old timber. I remembered passing by a stack of timber logs beside the highway. I said to Winnie, "Let's find out who the owner is, and maybe we can buy it."

After we learned who the owner was, I went over to his house. I spotted a man and a younger kid working on a tractor. I approached them and asked, "Is that your timber lying down by the highway?"

He said, "Yes, it is. Why do you ask?"

I responded, "Do you want to sell it?"

I told him my summer house had suffered a fire and I needed to rebuild it back to its original state. He looked at me with surprise and asked, "Sören! Is that you?"

"Yes!" I said.

"I am Lennart! I know you from the 1960s Saturday night dance at the folk house here in Mockfjärd. I knew many of you guys from Borlänge. You used to park your American cars in the front. Yeah, I remember you very well!" he said. Then we started talking about the old wild times.

He said, "Because it is you, I am going to give you a good deal. Come back in a couple of days and I'll let you know how much I want for the timber."

In the meantime, I called Krister, an old friend of mine I had met in California in 1977. He had actually worked for me in my window cleaning business. When he came back to Sweden, he took a course in timber building, so he came over and gave me an idea of what it would cost for a pile of timber like that. He said, "This is old, hard timber. If you can get this for 20,000 crowns, you've got a very good deal."

Well, I went back to Lennart the next day and asked him how much he wanted for the timber. To my great delight, he said, "I have another stack of timber with the same amount. You can have all of it for 10,000 crowns. And because we are friends, I will deliver it to your house."

"WOW! Thank you!" I exclaimed.

I called Krister and told him the good news. He told me that if he had known how much Lennart was willing to sell the timber for, he would have bought it himself. Lennart delivered the timber to our property, but I still hadn't found a company to help me rebuild our house. Everybody was so busy. Most of the companies said they could come and help us in September. It was May, and I needed to have the roof on before the first snow came, and I returned to California. I started to get a little bit worried, but one day, I went to the city, and on my way out of the gas station, I noticed a pickup truck outside with carpenter signage on it. So I waited for the driver outside, and soon, a young man came out. I asked him if he was the owner of the company, and he said, "No, I'm working for this company."

I told him that I needed some help, and he said, "Call my boss. The company is not far from your property."

I called the owner and, to my pleasant surprise, he said they could start the following day! He came over the next day to assess the project, and the following day, they started the work. We were able to replace the timber and put a new roof on the upstairs floor in three months. I worked with them from 7:00 a.m. to 4:30 p.m. every day. They would leave at that time, but I continued to work until I went to bed. Winnie helped me every day with anything she could do. She worked so hard. We needed some big beams for the ceiling, so I cut down big fern trees that were on our property, cleaned off the bark, and we later installed them upstairs.

Well, soon, three months ended, and it was time for Winnie to go home to California. Americans can only stay in Sweden for 90 days without a visa. So, I went to the immigration offices and had my visa extended for one more month. I needed to put down the concrete foundation for the front room of the house before I went back to California. I needed to have it done so it could set until the summer and be ready for the new timber construction. Well, I got it done with the help of my neighbor Tomas. It was a miracle that we got everything accomplished before I went back to California.

Our home on fire in 2020.

Winnie and I rebuilding together.

Preparing the ceiling beams.

Our remodeled home in 2023.

2020: The Lord is My Anesthesia

Ever since I went to the dentist for the first time as a teenager, I hated to have my mouth numbed because my cheek felt so terrible afterward. I even bit myself. So, after that, I had all my dental work done without anesthesia. I remember the first time I went to the dentist here in Palm Desert to have a wisdom tooth removed. I told the dentist I didn't want any anesthesia. He said, "You're crazy! The only other person who refused to be numbed before oral surgery was a guy from Denmark. What is it with you Vikings? You guys must love pain."

Well, through the years, I've had a few root canals, and I've also had some wisdom teeth pulled without anesthesia. One of my buddies said to me, "Why don't you videotape it next time?"

So I did! It's really a funny video. The doctor is super nervous, and he is begging me to change my mind before he starts his procedure. I am in a hurry to get back to our company to celebrate Thanksgiving with our employees. If you don't believe me, you can watch the whole thing on YouTube. Search for "THE LORD is My Anesthesia" by Mr. Samuels.

2020: Introducing the S-Arm

One day, I was sitting at a restaurant, and all of a sudden, a man came up and asked me, "Are you Mr. Sörbo?"

"Yes I am," I answered.

"My name is Armando. Sir, I've always wanted to meet you, and here you are! I've been using Sörbo products for many years. I have a tool that I invented that will eliminate detailing. I have personally been using it for some time now. I would like to show it to you."

After listening to him explain this new device, I realized that he had something very interesting. So we went out to his pickup truck, and he showed me a T-bar with a plastic rod on each end. He demonstrated the washer on the window, and I could see the benefit immediately. I thought it was a great idea, and to make a long story short, I purchased his idea. I immediately made a prototype from our T-bars. After using it for a couple of days, I realized I had to modify it because the plastic rods were in the center of the T-bar, so when I cleaned a window that had a very low frame, the arm slipped over the frame. To remedy the problem, I offset the arm on the end plug so it ended up closer to the window, and it performed exactly as I expected. This is an example of how and why experienced window cleaners have the advantage and ability to develop new products.

I am a professional window cleaner with 50 years of experience in the industry. I have the knowledge to work with the tools we create before we introduce them to the window cleaning market, and I know that this device reduces time because the arm separates the washer a quarter-inch from the window frame. Another feature of this tool is that when you use the Sörbo 3 × 4 Adjustable Wide-Body squeegee, holding it at a certain angle, a tiny little bit of water automatically goes back to the frame, just enough to clean it, but not enough so that you have to detail. This is the first improvement on a T-bar since it was invented in the '70s.

One of my final concerts in Palm Desert, with Garden
Fellowship, before COVID-19 struck the world.

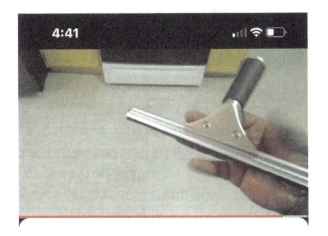

Description   ✕

**NEW FROM SÖRBO The Godfather
of the Widebody presents Ultra light
45 Sponsored by SÖRBO PRODUCTS**

 M.A.W. Masters At Wagtail

11	**316**	**2020**
Likes	Views	Dec 31

M.A.W. Short Trailer Teaser This tool is one
of the lightest of it's kind. Ultra light 45

Markus   the Window Cleaner
the t Burth the Nam Godfater
of the wide Body Sqnoegee,

My colleague coining my nickname "The Godfather" at the end of 2020.

2021: American Window Cleaner Magazine Highlights Sörbo, *the Godfather of the Wide-Body Squeegee*

In 2021, I was honored to appear in *American Window Cleaner Magazine.* My dedication, work, ideas, and inventions, which span over five decades, were highlighted in the March 2021 issue. The article on the cover page recognizes me as the Godfather of the Wide-Body Squeegee. My impact on the window cleaning industry was highlighted in three issues of the magazine: issues 215 through 217. Here are a few quotes from the magazine.

"What Sörbo brought to the Window Cleaning Industry has, and always will, benefit many window cleaners for years to come. As they say, 'anything Sörbo touches turns to Gold!'... he knew that those willing would likewise be profitable with Sörbo Window Cleaning Equipment. Sörbo — 'doing it smarter and in less time.' Who knows what is to come from SÖRBO in the 21st century . . . ?" — *AWC*

2021: My Mom Passed Away In Sweden, May 10

On May 4, 2021, we had a call from my brother in Sweden. He told me that Mom was ready to go home to be with the Lord Jesus very soon. So I called the nurse, and she told me that I should come home right away, and the doctor sent me a letter stating my mom's situation. With the letter from the doctor, we were able to get a special visa from the Swedish embassy to go to Sweden.

It took us four days to get to Sweden because of the COVID-19 epidemic, which made everything so complicated. What is truly frustrating is that it seems, as of 2023, that many of the policies and mandates which our governments forced upon us, including the wearing of masks, were ineffective in preventing the spread of this disease.

On Saturday, May 8, 2021, we arrived at our summerhouse in Sweden. On Sunday morning, we went to see my mom. All the nurses said my mom was waiting for me, and that kept her alive. When I walked into her room where she was lying, she was smiling. She looked so happy to see me and Winnie. I hugged her and told her I loved her. We stayed there all day Sunday, and that night, on Monday morning at 2:00 a.m., she took her last breath. We were blessed to have made it in time to be at her side until the end.

The next day, we started to work on the house. I had already arranged to have the timber fitted together by Allan Trogen, a professional timber specialist whom I got to know. Together with the truck driver, who was driving a truck with a hydraulic lift, we raised the new section in two days. Then, we put the plywood and the tar paper on the new section. After that, I managed to do the work myself. I had been trying to find old windows that would match the style of the house. I needed nine of them to finish the house. It was very difficult to find so many windows that would match. We had been praying really hard that God would find what we needed.

I had a neighbor below my property: a biker like me named Stefan. He came by to see how everything was going every now and then. I asked him if he might know somebody who had some old windows. I had looked in the classified ads for old windows, but no one was selling nine windows. One day, my biker friend came up to my house when I was working, and he said, "I've got something I want to show you; come with me."

I said, "What is it? Don't tell me you have some windows."

He just kept smiling and said, "Come, follow me."

He led me down to his house, and in my mind I was thinking, *Lord, I hope he has some windows.*

Well, I came down to his storage shack, and as soon as he opened the door, I spotted a whole bunch of windows. He said, "I purchased these windows, and I was going to use them for my house when I remodeled it. But as you can see, they are brown. My wife wanted to have white frames, so I can't use them. These are the sizes you need, and there are nine of them."

So I asked him, "How much do you want for these windows?"

He said, "Because it is you, you can have them for 1,000 crowns," which today is $95. That didn't even pay for the delivery.

These were double-paned insulated windows and the exact number that I had prayed for. On top of that, they also had the antique look — exactly what I needed for my house. I hope you realize by now that I believe that if you ask, you will receive. God is an awesome friend to have. He provides. I suppose many of you expected a totally different picture of Mr. Sörbo. This is the main reason I wanted to write the book. I am very happy with my life, and I love what I'm doing.

The rest of the time, I worked from 6:00 a.m. until we went to bed every day for four months. My other neighbor had scaffolding that I could borrow, so that was provided, too. Some days, we went to the secondhand store and purchased the most beautiful antique furniture, and we always found what we needed. It was a miracle, as was everything that happened that summer. My beautiful wife helped me a lot through the summer.

I've tried to keep the house's original look from 1890. The previous owner had installed a different front door. Looking at the picture that the shoemaker — the original builder — took, I could see that the original front door was a double door. I wanted to bring that look back. A few years earlier, I had looked on the internet and found a double door that matched the original doors. The only difference was that this door had a window in the upper panel. Otherwise, they looked exactly the same. I got them from an old railroad station that was remodeled in Ludvika a couple of years earlier. I cleaned and repainted those doors and made new frames, and I was planning to install those in the section that had burned down. I am grateful that I didn't because the front doors would have burned, too. To find a door from the 1800s that is exactly the same is also a miracle. I had it safely stored in the garage, and now it is installed in the new section, and it looks really good.

Well, we had a lot of work to do. We had to remove the floors in the whole house and remove all the old insulation, which was sawdust. After the fire department had done its job, however, it was soaking wet. I had to install the floor planks, which I special-ordered to match the original thickness. When I finished that, I ordered a stairway that led up to the bedroom so we could finally sleep inside the house at the end of the summer. We no longer had to sleep in our trailer, which was okay but a little crowded. I finally installed the rest of the electrical system, so we had lights in the new living room section. We had been looking for a chandelier for this new room, which is two stories high, up to the ceiling. However, none of the ones we looked at were big enough for this room. I was also looking for a wood-burning stove that would match that old-style house, and I wanted to install it in the corner. But we couldn't find anything original. So I said, "Maybe we can find something when we get back to California."

As soon as we came back home, we went out to a second-hand store looking for a chandelier. They had really beautiful chandeliers, but they were so expensive, and I didn't really find what I was looking for. They all cost over $2,000. I had a feeling that He would help me to find something for a lot lower cost, and even though they cost so much, they weren't really the style that would work in that old house. While I was walking around in the store, I spotted a little storage room, and in there, I spotted a beautiful chandelier that would be perfect. So I walked out to the front and told the salesperson, "I found a chandelier. Can you come and help me?"

He followed me over and said, "Well that's the one we had in the old store, and it is kind of bent up a little bit here and there."

But it was exactly what I had been looking for. He said, "It's not in the showroom so I have to ask the manager if he wants to sell it."

He asked me, "How much can you offer?"

So I told him, "I'll give you $200 cash."

"Let me ask him," he said.

When he came back, he said, "You can have it for $250."

I did not expect to hear that! Another miracle happened! "Thank you, Lord."

When I came home, I started looking for a wood-burning stove on the internet, and I found one on eBay. It was located in the state of Virginia, and it was a Round Oak from 1907, in excellent original condition. So, I purchased it, and as soon as I received it in California, I shipped it to Sweden. You probably don't think that much about it, but when you have a good friend who's looking out for you, it's really cool because it seems like things just happen. The more I dig into my past, the more I realize that God saved me so I could share His goodness with you. I'm nobody special, as you've probably discovered already. All these things have happened because 23 years ago, I decided to live for Him, and this is why He is present all the time.

2021: Introducing the 45-Degree Viper

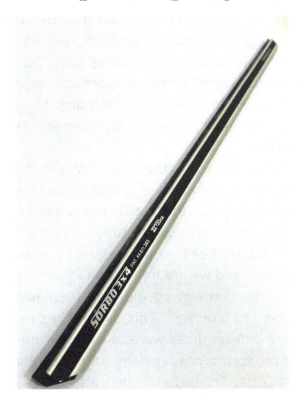

Sörbo's Viper, designed in 2020.

One day, I heard about a window cleaner in Australia who had modified my Sörbo 3 × 4 adjustable wide-body Quicksilver channel. His name was Herman Weiland. So, I looked at his website, and I realized he had made the modifications seven years earlier, in 2014. He had actually removed the front of my 40-degree angle, and I liked what I saw. I realized it would be really cool to make a 45-degree angle squeegee. So I called Mr. Weiland, and we talked on the phone for an hour. Since he was also a professional window cleaner and an inventor, we had mutual interests. Today, most of the window cleaning manufacturers have never cleaned windows professionally themselves, so it is really exciting to talk to people with experience and knowledge more deeply. I later found that Mr. Weiland had been inventing a lot of different products. I told him that I was interested in developing a new channel using his idea. I had an idea for a new model called the Viper and I wanted to pay him for his idea. He told me to give the money to some charity that I thought was good. So, I donated the money to the schools in the Philippines.

The Sörbo Viper became the seventh model of the Sörbo 3 × 4 Adjustable Wide-Body arsenal of squeegees. I also designed a totally new end clip with the first 45-degree angle for this new squeegee model. When I do something, I make it in stainless steel, not in plastic. I believe professional window cleaners like high quality, and we are here to serve them. In order to manufacture this new squeegee design, I also had to design new equipment to produce it. This is why I like this business.

But more difficult times were to come for our company because of the coronavirus epidemic. Many companies went under, and Sörbo Products Inc. was affected in a big way. Namely, our ability to produce squeegees was significantly hampered because the manufacturer who produced the rubber — our most important product — was not available to us for over a year and a half. But, because I had developed the silicone squeegee blade in 1994, we stayed in business.

Throughout the pandemic, we sold the silicone blades in 50-foot rolls, but because of this setback, we started to cut sizes and sold them in dozen and gross amounts. Personally, I like silicone, even though it has a little bit of a different feel compared to the natural synthetic rubber. Of course, the silicone is what is used in the biggest squeegee in the world, the Sörbo Eliminator 3 × 4 Adjustable Wide-Body squeegee. In sizes up to 78 inches (195 cm), it has proven to be a very good squeegee rubber.

Besides, it works right out of the box; you don't have to break it in. Combined with the Sörbo Glide washing detergent and the cleaning powder, it works great on any window. It's very smooth and adapts to the glass with a minimum amount of pressure. Also, this material does not get stiff in temperatures below zero like natural and synthetic rubber does in winter time when it must be swapped with soft rubber. The other benefit of using silicone rubber blades is that you can cut the blades to size yourself, so you don't have any waste. We realized that when people have the chance to try the silicone for the first time, many of them keep buying it. This was good for our business during a difficult time.

Thankfully, our rubber vendor recovered, and we are back in business. We are now filling back orders from 2021, and the problem is behind us. We are back to producing the highest quality squeegee rubber on the market again. I found out from the big window cleaning companies that our squeegee rubber holds up for nine days. With that quality and durability, it is actually better and less expensive to buy high quality.

2022: Introducing the Cobra Flipper

My buddy kept bugging me about inventing a new flipper that works correctly. He pointed out the one that was already on the market, and he was sure I could invent something that would work better. So, finally, I decided to take a look at the ones on the market, and I realized they were all attached to the squeegee handle. I did not think that was a good idea. I could see how to improve the performance by inventing a new design, and because of the work I had done on our Cobra channel with the plastic end plugs in 1994, I realized that I could invent a totally new product with a new concept. My idea was a new, separate clip made of spring steel that would be designed with the right pressure so that you could insert it into the Cobra squeegee channel, and of course, it would also fit the Silverado 3 × 4 channel. I improved the rods, which were very flimsy and made of plastic. I designed it with a quarter-inch rigid aircraft aluminum rod instead. I wanted to make a kit so the window cleaners didn't have to buy a new handle grip or a new squeegee. I designed it so they could easily snap it onto the squeegee channel they already had. Today, you can buy the Sörbo flipper kit separately and snap it on or off really quickly.

Sörbo's Flipper, invented and patented in 2022.

Soon after that, we started to advertise the new Cobra Flipper. The window cleaners who are using only the Sörbo 3 × 4 adjustable Quicksilver wide-body squeegee kept asking if the Flipper fit their channel, but it did not fit in a secure way because it was a different design. I realized I had to design a new squeegee model again for these people so they would be happy.

2022: Introducing the Q-Cobra 3 × 4 Adjustable Wide-Body Squeegee

Sörbo's Quicksilver Squeegee.

In the month of August, 2022 we introduced the Q-Cobra 3 × 4 Adjustable Wide-Body squeegee. This was the brother of the Quicksilver squeegee. As soon as we came up with the Cobra Flipper, window cleaners kept asking if it would fit the Quicksilver channel. I realized that it did not fit securely, so I decided to make a special squeegee channel that would perform the same way as the Quicksilver, especially for the flipper. So, I removed the end plugs on the Cobra and cut each end 40 degrees, exactly like the Quicksilver. To test our new Q-Cobra, we had a handful of window cleaners trying it out for a few weeks before we released it, and they all liked it very much. So, on August 27, 2022, Sörbo introduced the eighth model of squeegees in our arsenal, the Q-Cobra.

2022: Teaching Window Cleaners How to Use the Sörbo 3 × 4 Adjustable Wide-Body Squeegees

Through the years, I have held dozens of window-cleaning seminars all over the world. In 1987, the window cleaners were amazed when they saw my 36-inch Sörbo 3 × 4 Adjustable Wide-Body squeegee for the first time. Most people doubted that a squeegee of that size would ever work. But because of my new revolutionary design, every angle on the channel makes a difference. It became the most rigid squeegee on the market. Some window cleaners were laughing when they first looked at it. One guy said, while laughing, "What am I going to use that long stick for? I could kill somebody with that."

This was one of the students in my seminar, and I had the opportunity to teach him how to operate this new squeegee. When I had the opportunity to show the window cleaners hands-on, they got very excited. Most of them ended up buying our squeegees at the seminar. The majority of the window cleaners I was teaching used the slalom method, or the fanning method, as some people call it. You start in one of the upper corners, and then you go over to the opposite corner, and then you start to go back and forth from side to side. Basically, you build a bow shape in the middle of the window, and you actually cross that back and forth until you come to the bottom of the window. This is one of the reasons I invented the wide-body squeegee. If you clean a sliding glass door that is 8.5 feet high and 3.5 feet wide with a standard 18-inch squeegee, your hand will travel somewhere between 28 and 32 feet per sliding glass door. If you clean 200 sliding doors a day, you are moving your hand around 6,000 feet a day. But, if you use a 36-inch Sörbo 3 × 4 Adjustable Wide-Body squeegee, and pull three horizontal strokes, you travel 10.5 feet on each window, and that is only 2,100 feet a day. Using our large squeegee, you reduce the distance by two-thirds.

Next time you're cleaning a window, follow your hand and record every 12 inches you move your hand across a window. You'll be surprised. Ever since I changed the window cleaning industry, and introduced this simple technique, many window cleaners have actually called me and told me that the pain they had had in their elbows, shoulders, and wrists for years had suddenly disappeared. This was because of the wide-body squeegee that I invented.

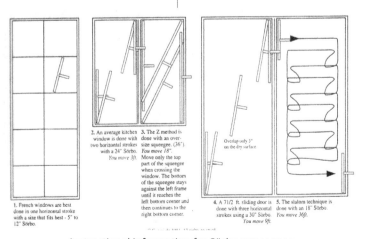

SÖRBO POINTERS

SÖRBO 3x4 is the only squeegee made in sizes from 5" to 50". This is the longest, strongest, straightest squeegee and the only squeegee with three patents at the same time - Design, Adjustment and End Plug.

(See Channel on front page)
A standard squeegee has only one setting while the Sörbo has 5 settings.

1. By moving the squeegee rubber from the No.1 position to the second setting the rubber becomes softer and will adapt better to to an uneven window. For the first time, windows can be cleaned up to the 4th. floor. We also developed a 40 foot extension pole that weighs just 12 pounds.

2. The new T-shaped Sörbo rubber fits most channels on the market and when used in a Sörbo adjustable squeegee the rubber can be resharpened 3 times in each of the four settings. This means that you can sharpen a Sörbo rubber 12 times and save 93% of your present cost.

3. This unique squeegee has a 40 degree angle in each end so you can clean closer into the corners and the frame, resulting in less detailing.

4. Today a store front can be cleaned in 1/3rd. the time it takes with a conventional squeegee. With the right size Sörbo, labor can be reduced and time cut in half. (With the Z Method) The new Safety handle and the new Fast Release handle are universal and fit any squeegee on the market. With the reset Fast Release and the smooth lower jaw, this makes the safest handle on the market, particularly, the Safety handle with the outlet for the safety line.

Do you know how many feet a professional window cleaner moves his arm a day with the conventional method? Example: Average 200 panels a day with the fanning technique and an 18" squeegee, you move your arm 7200 feet a day. With a 30" Sörbo 3x4 Squeegee, the same amount is done by moving your arm just 1/4th or 2400 feet.

1. French windows are best done in one horizontal stroke with a size that fits best - 5" to 12" Sörbo.

2. An average kitchen window is done with two horizontal strokes with a 24" Sörbo. *You move 3ft.*

3. The Z method is done with an over-size squeegee. (36"). *You move 18".* Move only the top part of the squeegee when crossing the window. The bottom of the squeegee stays against the left frame until it reaches the left bottom corner and then continues to the right bottom corner.

4. A 7 1/2 ft. sliding door is done with three horizontal strokes using a 30" Sörbo. *You move 9ft.*

5. The slalom technique is done with an 18" Sörbo. *You move 36ft.*

Overlap only 3" on the dry surface.

Instructional information for Sörbo squeegees.

The second technical aspect of my invention is the adjustment in the squeegee channel, and that can also eliminate fatigue. By moving the squeegee rubber to the second setting from the bottom, you reduce the pressure needed to remove the water from the window, and through the years, I always demonstrated how I put my little finger in the handle of the 36-inch Sörbo 3 × 4 to clean the window. This adjustable technology in my channels reduces the pressure up to 90 percent. It takes less pressure to use a 36-inch Sörbo 3 × 4 Adjustable Wide-Body squeegee than a standard squeegee, and the second advantage with the adjustments is that you can resharpen your squeegee up to 12 times and save a bundle of money, instead of buying 12 new squeegee rubbers.

2023: Introducing the Grizzly Scrubber

It was time again to upgrade our scrubber sleeve. I was talking to a window cleaner, and he mentioned that you have to press a little bit too hard when you're scrubbing the window, so we had been looking at new material. We found one that is a lot thicker than the original and would work really well for the Grizzly scrubber. We saw it the same way, and it turned out to be a very efficient scrubber because of the heavy material. They are a little bit banana-shaped, but they will stretch out when you put them on the T-bar.

In Closing ...

Me today, with all of my patents, as well as the American Window Cleaner Magazine (AWC Magazine) featuring me on the cover.

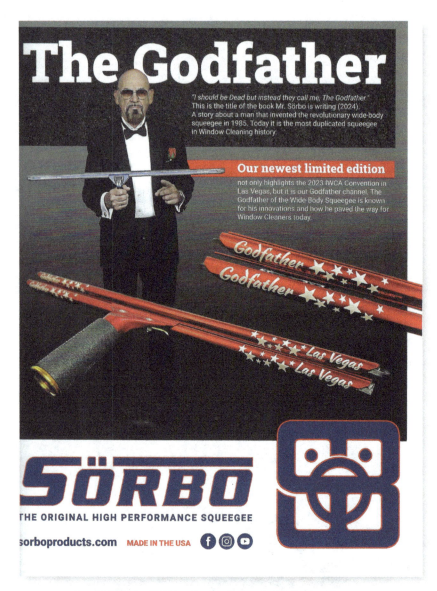

Our 2023 limited edition "revolutionary" wide-body squeegee.
An ad from AWC Magazine in which I was on the cover.

How to Operate a 36-Inch Sörbo 3 × 4 Adjustable Wide-Body Squeegee

If you're a beginner, I'd like to teach you how to operate the 36-inch Sörbo 3 × 4 Adjustable Wide-Body squeegee, and I want you to start out with straight horizontal strokes. During the 37 years I've been teaching people, I have seen how they react the first time they try my wide-body squeegee, and 90 percent of the time, they do it the same way they do with an 18-inch squeegee. So, therefore, I will now explain it in a very simple way. Let's say you are pulling a trailer. You are always ahead of it, but if you back up and push the trailer, it is a lot harder to steer it, and you can lose control. It's the same thing with my wide-body squeegee: if you hold the squeegee with your right hand, always start on the left side of the window, and if you're left-handed, then start on the opposite side. Spread your legs and then lean your upper body toward the left side so you are facing the left frame.

So this is how you start. (It will be the opposite way if you're left-handed.) With your right hand, start by pressing the squeegee in toward the vinyl seal that surrounds the glass. And pull the squeegee a quarter of an inch, and then go back to where you started. Tap the window frame twice; that way, you have a dry start. As soon as you leave the frame, lead with the top of the squeegee around 3 degrees, and then you start to lean your body all over to the right side, still pulling the squeegee. You will find that you are pulling the squeegee all the way to the right frame. If you've done it right, then your hand will never pass your face; it should always be on the left side of your nose. (Remember the trailer: if you start to pass your nose, then you start pushing the squeegee instead of pulling it.)

If the window is wider, you have to start to walk. As soon as you come to the right frame, you turn your body back toward your left and twist the squeegee handle so the rubber blade acts like your tongue, and lick the water off the window at the same time as you remove the squeegee. If you're left-handed, you do the same procedure the opposite way. If you have a very long window, start walking beside the window, and always lead with the top of the squeegee at around 3 degrees, like a ski jumper when they take off from the ramp, so that you never leave a streak.

Now, go back and repeat until you reach the bottom. Overlap on the dry surface no more than 2 inches. These are the basics when you start practicing with the Sörbo 3 × 4 Adjustable Wide-Body squeegee. Once you get the basics, you start to relax, and you will manage to do it without even thinking about it.

The other thing you need to adjust is the angle on your handle. Move it in and out until you feel it glide easiest. If you have the handle too close to the window, the squeegee rubber will go flat and it will leave a film of water. If you go too far out, then the rubber will scatter and make a noise. But after a few windows, you will actually get a feel for it, and it will work really well. Remember, practice does wonders.

I know some of you will come up with your own ideas, and that is okay as long as it works for you. Because I was the first person to use a 36-inch squeegee, I had to come up with new techniques. And I have been demonstrating many of them through the years. I have been doing it since 1975 when I invented the wide-body squeegee. My goal through the years has been to help window cleaners reduce labor and injuries and increase their profit. Proof of that is the squeegee blade sharpener. Some people have asked me, "Don't you sell less squeegee rubber when you sell the Docket squeegee blade sharpener, especially when you can sharpen the blade 12 times?"

I tell them, "Obviously we are going to reduce sales of squeegee blades, but it has a small impact on our profits because we sell a lot of squeegee rubbers. I believe when you are helping the window cleaners to increase productivity and save money, you get it back in many ways."

I always wanted to be there for the window cleaners. Whenever I can develop the tools that can save them time, that's a big reward for me and our company. When I first came up with the idea to invent the first 36-inch squeegee, which reduced two-thirds of labor and a lot of stress on your wrists, elbows, and shoulders, I had people calling our office, and I listened to them express how grateful they were for my products. The stories they told about how they were able to be free of the pain they had for many years once they started to use the Sörbo 3 × 4 adjustable squeegee was the most rewarding thing for me.

I think it is similar to my new life in Christ. When I became a born-again Christian, so much of the inner pain I had been living with was swept away when I began to live my life differently. My hope is that you will also experience some of the miracles that happened to me in this book. I have been invited to speak at the IWCA window cleaning convention banquet a couple of times, and I always had the opportunity to share my faith. A few years back, I received an IWCA Lifetime Achievement Award. That meant a lot to me. I had the opportunity to tell everyone present about all my inventions, and I had the opportunity to sing two Christian songs. So that was really awesome! And then, COVID-19 came.

Inventing a New Product

Through the years, I have had a couple of window cleaners contact me with inventions. I've always told them, "You make more money if you make a prototype, have a machine shop make the parts, market it yourself, and sell it directly to the window cleaning industry." I tell them that I have a few inventions that I haven't even started to make yet. If you sent me your invention, and suppose I told you I already had the same invention in my book, would you believe me? This is why I have never taken on or even wanted to look at an invention that a window cleaner talked to me about. The only exception I have ever made was when I met the window washer who invented the ARM washer. That was the only time I have ever taken on somebody's idea. The reason I did so was because he showed me that he actually had a sample of his idea that worked right there at the restaurant. If you sign it over to the manufacturing company, they have to make money, and you make maybe 7 percent of the wholesale price. That will not add up to very much.

I have one window cleaning friend named Jerry Rigdon, who has been successful with his products. He asked me many years ago about an idea for an invention, and I suggested the same thing to him. Jerry is the inventor of the ledger, and he has been marketing that item since 1995, one year after I invented my Twin Ledge Angle. Jerry even told me he got the idea because of my 3 × 4 adjustable squeegee; you can go all the way down to the bottom frame without leaving water.

As you know already from my history, you don't have to be educated to develop a new product in your industry. I'm sure many of you have already ended up in a situation where you couldn't finish a window with the equipment you already had. Maybe you have already started to think about an easier way to do it. That's how many of my invention ideas came to me. And as a manufacturer in window cleaning equipment, we have a greater advantage. The next thing you do is to take a piece of paper and make a rough drawing of what you think the product would look like. This is just the starting point. If you're like me, a total failure in school, you probably have some other gifts. You can make a prototype or have somebody make one for you. And then try it! That's when the adjustments start. Keep changing the angles and the dimensions until it works perfectly. Don't overlook that every little angle on the product can change the performance more than you think. You have now completed one-third of the project.

The next thing I did was to look at all the parts. If the parts are too difficult to produce, then I change the design until I reduce the labor cost to make that part. Or, perhaps make a simpler mold for a plastic part. If you have a few parts, then you have to work through each one of them if it is possible to reduce the cost. You also have to think about the strength of the material you use to make the individual parts so the product does not break when people start using it. Once you've got all that written down, you can make a print and send it to a machine shop, extrusion company, or injection molding company to get estimates from three different manufacturers for each part. Once you receive all the pricing, you have to figure out the labor costs and whether you have to drill holes, cut lengths, or polish some of these products. You also have to calculate the labor costs to produce the product. You must also include any labels or screen printing that will be placed on the final product. Last of all, you must take into account the cost of packaging materials like cartons and boxes, shrink-wrapping, or special packaging. When you calculate all those numbers, that will be your manufacturing cost for the product.

However, in order to sell it to a distributor, you must mark up your production cost four to five times, depending on the margins you are shooting for when the item is finally sold on the market. So, if the product cost you $5.00 to produce, you must multiply that by 4. $5.00 × 4 = $20.00. That will be the retail cost. If you sell directly to the end user, you would have a profit of $15.00. However, if you sell it to a distributor, you give them 50 percent off your retail price. This will leave you with a $5.00 profit. So you have made a 100 percent markup profit from your cost, which was $5.00 dollars.

How I Started My Window Cleaning Business

How do you start the window cleaning business? Through the years, I have been doing seminars all over the world, teaching professionals and non-professionals how to clean windows. In one of my seminars, I even had an attorney who wanted to start cleaning windows. He said he was not happy in his profession. So, he wanted to look into the window-cleaning industry. I don't know if he became a window cleaner or not, but for the average person, it is not very expensive to start a window-cleaning business. You can buy a Sörbo window cleaning kit for under $500.00. The amazing thing is that if you do things right, you can make $50 to $100,000 a year with that kit and by watching the videos that I have posted on YouTube. There, you can learn the different techniques that I invented over the past 50 years in the window cleaning industry.

One video is called the Z method. In this video, we show how you can clean a small residential account very easily with the 36-inch squeegee. There is a second video called the upside-down L method. In that video, we teach you how you can reach higher than you would believe with the 36-inch Sörbo 3 × 4

Adjustable Wide-Body squeegee. There is a third video, which we call the upside-down U method, which helps you become a very fast window cleaner, as you can see in one of the videos where I'm doing a race with the guy who used an 18-inch squeegee. Yes, I said he did two passes, and I'm done already.

But the question most people asked me is, "How do you get the first customer?"

I will give you the answer to that question shortly. Just keep reading this book to the end. When I started cleaning windows in 1971, the window cleaning industry was not a very highly respected business. However, I hope that, in reading my book, you have noticed that my goal was to do everything with excellence. Whether I cleaned a window or introduced a new product to the industry, I wanted to make a difference in how people perceived the window cleaning industry. The reason for this is that when I started cleaning windows, most window cleaners were walking around in jeans, a wrinkled T-shirt, and dirty tennis shoes that used to be white. I wanted to be different, so the first thing I did was to purchase uniforms, which I wore every day that I worked. I got blue pants, a white button-down shirt with blue stripes, and nice shiny black shoes. I purchased six sets, so I had a clean uniform every day. Winnie did the laundry at the end of the week, and she ironed every uniform. In my seminars, I used to say, "Whenever we arrive for a job, we look like a million bucks!"

When we started to get accounts in large homes with beautiful carpets or tiled floors, I realized it was not good for us to clean a client's windows while leaving their carpets or tiles dirty. So, soon after that, I came up with the idea to use hospital covers for our shoes. That was a great hit! The customers noticed that we really cared about their floors, and the word spread to their friends and family. We got more work by word of mouth.

Later on, I invented the high bucket stand (the Quatropod), which is a tremendously good workstation that you can bring along inside and outside the house. When the customers opened the door and saw all the new equipment we carried, they were amazed. I still remember arriving at a new customer's home for the first time. The husband opened the door, looked at us, and said to his wife, "Come and look at these guys and the equipment they have! I've never seen anything like it!"

So the first thing I recommend you do, if you're serious about starting a window cleaning business, is that you buy the equipment, start cleaning your own windows, and look at the videos on YouTube at www.sorboproducts.com and Superb Window Cleaning. There, you can see Sörbo products being demonstrated the right way. Then practice, practice, and practice some more.

When you learn to apply the right amount of pressure and the right angle of the handle, keep in mind that if you move the rubber blade to the second setting in the channel, you need to turn the handle away from the window more. This is something you get the feel of when you practice. The biggest mistake beginners make with the 36-inch Sörbo 3 × 4 Adjustable Wide-Body squeegee is that they use too much pressure, so practice that until you feel comfortable. The quality comes out 100 percent. Remember to master the different techniques.

Once you have done the above, now you are ready to get yourself a nice uniform. Print up some business cards. Then go down to the grocery store where all the homeowners are going, or the shopping center on a Saturday, and ask a store owner if you can clean the storefronts for free. If you can, find a place where the people are walking in and out all day long. I can assure you that if you look better than the window cleaner they already have, they will come and ask you if you can come by their house and give an estimate. You can do that anytime, but if they want to schedule you for window cleaning right away, bring along with you a weekly schedule book. Ask them when they would like you to come by. If they say Monday morning, look in your schedule book and give them two dates to choose from; that way, you appear to be a very busy window cleaner. When you arrive at their home, you can ask them if they want the mirrors done also.

I always start counting the windows on the outside; that way, you don't miss any windows. Count each panel, which means each window with a frame around it. Old homes have two panels in each window that you can open. At the same time, inspect for watermarks from sprinklers, and also slide your hand over the glass to feel if there is spray paint on the glass, which is very hard to see from the outside. And when you're done outside, go inside and start walking to the left, facing the front door, and do what I call following the wall system. That way, you do not miss any windows or mirrors in any room. When you're done, you should end up on the right side of the front entrance. This will be very important later when you get a helper working the outside while you do the inside.

Let's say you got the job, and now you're coming back to clean the windows on the date you scheduled. When you arrive at the customer's house, take all the equipment out of your truck or your van. Once you have a helper, they will fill up the water outside while you immediately bring your equipment inside. Start on the left side of the front door, open the windows, pop off the screens, and start vacuum-cleaning the tracks. At the same time, your helper should start brushing the screens and cleaning the windows on the outside in the same direction you are working on the inside. He is working to the right, facing the front door. When you are done vacuum-cleaning, take your bucket containing chemicals. Remember to only use our non-suds chemicals: the Sörbo window cleaning powder and the Sörbo Glide friction reducer. Remove the bucket from your Quadropod and fill up the water in the kitchen sink. By now, your partner should have already cleaned a few windows, so you can start cleaning the inside in the same direction they are going. This is when you inspect both the inside and the outside. Hopefully, your helper did a good job. If you find any marks, take your AAAA steel wool from the Sörbo pouch and remove marks or particles left on the window. It's always easier to inspect the window from the inside because you are doing more work on the inside when you add the mirrors.

Always remember to lay down two beach towels below the windows and sliding glass doors. Some of the homes have small windows called French windows, and there you can use the Sörbo multi-squeegee. You can do two or three of them in one pass. The multi-squeegee can be ordered in custom sizes for each account.

And when the outside window cleaner is done with cleaning and perhaps acid washing, water staining, or paint scraping, that's when they change the water in their bucket and add new window cleaning chemicals. Make sure your helper puts on their shoe covers (like I introduced in my videos in the '90s). Then they come in and help you finish up on the inside. (You can look at the end of the book for instructions on how to charge for windows and mirrors, paint scraping, and hard water stain removal.)

High-quality work is most important because you will get most of your new customers by word of mouth. Advertising your service with fliers and ads in the newspapers is not very efficient. You usually get the people who are looking for lower pricing from those sources. It will probably take a couple of seasons to fill up full weeks of work, so it helps if you can have a part-time job in the meantime. Keep going down to the grocery store and work for free on Saturdays. That's where you will pick up your first customers at the beginning of your new business because they can see the product they are buying when they look at what you are doing, and you can't get better advertising than that.

However, it is equally important to use the Sörbo chemicals that keep windows cleaner longer. That was one thing that customers asked us over and over again: "How come the windows stay clean so long when you clean them? They didn't do that when our other window cleaner serviced our windows!"

The very common reason is that the window cleaner used too much soap, and the second reason is that many of them use dishwashing soap. Both of these will leave residue on the window, which in time attracts pollution and makes the window get dirty quicker. Dishwashing compounds have hand-protection components, which also cling to the glass. If you do the windows regularly — let's say once a week for the high-end clients — it doesn't really matter because the windows are practically clean every time you go there. You have to have a very good window cleaner because if they don't do a good job, it will look worse when they leave and also, you have to be on top of it because some of the cleaners will skip windows, and I don't tolerate that. Like I said before, check that you can press the nylon seal at the bottom of the window. When you do that, water should come up between the seal and the glass, and you can tell if the window has been cleaned.

But the customer who recognizes how long the windows stay clean is the one whose windows you clean three or four times a year or less. These are usually higher-end clients. They will notice if the windows stay clean longer, and they are the ones who will refer you to their friends.

I also mentioned paint scraping. I had some bad experiences in the beginning, especially when you do a brand-new home, and the contractor has already cleaned the windows. Then, when the windows get dirty the next time, they call you. And what you have to do is inspect the windows really well because I have never found a home that doesn't have scratched windows, and you have to look at the home when the windows have been cleaned to be able to protect yourself and see that they don't blame you for the scratches. Every time I'm done with an assignment, and they agree, I'll tell them I want to do a test on the window to see if it's scratched. I ask them to come out when I do it. I clean a little portion and show them the scratches that are on the window already from the construction crew. At the same time, test the glass for an overspray of paint: slide your fingers over that clean surface; you can feel it if there's paint on it. That way, you have to charge more.

One more extra charge is hard water stain removal because sprinklers are constantly spraying on the glass, and you have alkaline on the glass that looks like a milky substance. This is tricky because if it is on for more than a year, then it gets deeper into the pores of the glass and is very difficult to remove, but whatever is on the surface comes off very easily with Sörbo hard water stain remover, which is the safest chemical on the market. It will not remove the color on the anodizing, but that is also an extra charge for that service.

Sometimes, you find that people have been repairing windows, and by mistake, they got silicone glue on their glass, and that is a nightmare to remove. The only thing that removes that is the Sörbo hard water stain remover, but in this case you don't use any water — you just apply the powder on the rag and wipe it in a circular movement over the silicone, and then you remove the rag and just blow the dust off the window with your mouth. The window will be totally clean, and you probably don't even need to wash it if you use a lot of breath when you blew the dust off.

Sörbo's Most Famous Training Videos

If you are a professional, an amateur, or a beginner using Sörbo equipment for the first time, I highly recommend that you learn the techniques from these videos first. You can purchase the DVD directly from Sorbo Products, Inc. or download it from our website: www.sorboproducts.com.

How to Charge for Window Cleaning

1. Vacuum cleaning the tracks: $5.00 per track, which includes two sliding glass panels.
2. Standard window cleaning costs: $10.00 for each panel. Very efficient with the 36-inch 3 × 4 Sörbo Adjustable Wide-Body squeegee.
3. French window cleaning with the multi-squeegee: $2.50 for each panel.
4. Every wardrobe mirror: $5.00 each.
5. Hard water stain removal: $20.00 per panel; efficient if you use the Sörbo hard water stain remover.
6. Paint scraping each window: $12 per panel; faster if you use the Sörbo 6-inch scraper.
7. Construction cleaning is not included in this. Costs could be higher.
8. Removing of silicone glue: $20.00 per panel; easily done with Sörbo hard water stain remover, applying it dry with a rag.

My Wife, My Pillar and My Partner

I have not had time to say enough about my best partner in life — my wife, Winnie. She has been a pillar in my life. You will know from the story earlier that God brought us together. We have been married for fifty years, and it doesn't seem like more than eight years. She has been such a faithful partner in my life. She has never been afraid of working hard. Through the years of cleaning windows together, she proved that she could do the same job the guys could do without complaining. I have never heard her complain. She's a very forgiving person. She must be because I'm still married to her. She went through very difficult times with me because of my early years of being a heavy drinker. After many nights being out drinking with the guys, coming home early in the morning, sometimes ending up in fights, and sometimes coming home with dirty clothes, still she never complained in an angry voice. On many occasions, it happened that her friends asked her why she was still with me, and she said she could see the light at the end of the tunnel.

And sometimes, when I woke up with a hangover on Sunday morning and asked her for a beer, she never answered in an angry voice. She very lovingly brought me a cold beer, but sometimes she pointed out it was not good for me. She explained later that if she had been fighting with me, it would have been even worse.

And it is because of her loving heart, shining through her cute face, that she is still as pretty as she was the first moment I saw her walking in at Moby's fifty years ago. Thank you, Lord Jesus.

I didn't know then, but I know now that she was right because when Jesus came into our lives, everything changed, and we started to have a refreshed relationship. I have always been a very worried person. Maybe that is why I always have to fix a problem before I go to bed. My wife is very strong. She never panics. She always tells me, "Don't worry. It will be fine. Take care of it tomorrow."

But when I look back at our life together, I know that what I have accomplished in my life is because of her being with me. That was the first thing I knew in 1987 when I asked her if we should start to manufacture our products, and we didn't have a clue where to start. I told her, "We might lose our house if we don't do it right."

I'll never forget her response. She said, "I believe in you."

My lovely wife, Winnie, has believed in me for almost fifty years. As a matter of fact, she believed in me more than I believed in myself many times, and I thank God for partnering me with a woman like her. Until the very end, in December of 2023, I would make her laugh as much as I could, and I told her every day how pretty she was, and she would look at me with that beautiful smile — the same as when I was blowing in her face on the dance floor, not so long ago. Love you, Winnie.

I am equally grateful for my daughter Mindi, whom my wife raised by herself, more or less, while I was too busy inventing.

Thank you to our daughter, Annette. She was involved with our company from the beginning, trying new inventions as I created them. I so appreciate your inspiring presence as I became an inventor.

I also want to thank our son, James, for the many years he was working in our window cleaning company. I was so proud of him when he won the window cleaning contest in Palm Desert where I had the opportunity to use the competition windows that I built.

Some Final Thoughts

From time to time through the years, window cleaners have asked me to write a book about my life. Six months ago, I got inspired to write this book. I thought I would write a book about Sören Sörbo Samuelsson and the road to becoming the greatest inventor in the window cleaning industry. I thought I would write about how I got the extraordinary name "Godfather of the Wide-Body Squeegee." The man who baptized me with that name a few years back was a very well-known window cleaner making videos on YouTube, Marcus Bey of Marcus Window Cleaning of New Jersey. I got to know him because a mutual friend introduced me to him. He was a very nice, friendly person, and he is greatly missed by all of us in the window cleaning industry. I didn't think about the title he gave me that much. It was more like a cliché. But later on, I realized that I should take advantage of that name because I am the only one who could claim a name like that. That came up just in time for this book, and that is what I expected this book would be about: the legacy of Mr. Sörbo.

The progress of turning my 1939 Caddy into a street rod.

Preparing one of the tires for my Caddy.

Getting tires ready for the Caddy!

The engine that I personally built for my Caddy.

Hard at work on the Caddy.

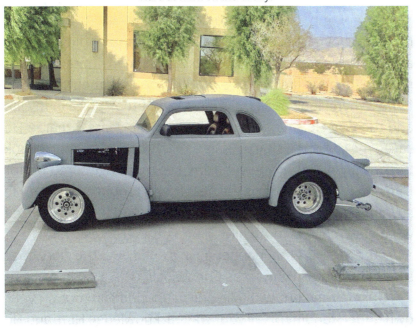

My street rod at the time of this writing. 1939 Cadillac LaSalle.

Standing by the product of my hard work.

But going back during corrections, I realized that God's hand is all over this book. He saved me from ending up with a headstone, and I started realizing how many miracles have happened in my life. I realize that this book is about faith and hope. When I look at all the miracles that took place in my life and the way He saved my life through the years, I realize He saved me so I could share His love in this book. The more I look back at my relationship with Him, the more I get fired up for Him and realize that He is the best friend I could ever have. He surrounded me with three Christian kids, and finally, I realized what was missing in my life. That is the greatest miracle of all — the miracles that happened in my life. And the glory goes to my Lord and Savior, Jesus Christ!

Trust in the Lord with all your heart, and lean not on your own understanding; in all your ways acknowledge Him, and He shall direct your paths. (Proverbs 3:5–6)

So, to end this book, I would like to thank my Lord and Savior for saving my life so many times. I'd like to thank my wife for her support through the years and for a wonderful marriage that God orchestrated. I want to thank all our children: Anette, James, Mindi, and our son-in-law, Bart, for bringing the Lord into our house so many years ago. And I am grateful for my grandson Markus Samuelsson Hernandez for being our new member of the Sorbo team!

Special thanks to all my employees who have been so faithful, producing the highest quality for so many years. Thanks to all the Sörbo window cleaners all over the world. Without you, we would not be here. My thanks go out to George Brady, and to David Gonzalez, Jr., who has been correcting the grammar in my book, and to Kathy Rodriguez, who spiced up the book with the title. Finally, I'd like to thank Best Seller Publishing for launching this book.

God bless you all!
Mr. Sörbo

To see nearly 200 of my paintings and listen to my music as well, please visit www.creativeartbysorbo.com

And to see current Sörbo products, please visit www.sorboproducts.com

Special Thanks

George Brady — Editing & Proofreading

David Gonzalez, Jr. — Editing & Proofreading

Christina Gonzalez — All around office assistance :)

Kathy Rodriguez — My book title

Matthew Schnarr and the BSP Team —
Editing, Design, and Publishing

About the Author

Before Sörbo Samuelsson invented the 3×4® Adjustable squeegee channel, aka the Wide-Body Squeegee, everyone thought the squeegee had reached the pinnacle of perfection, that it didn't need improvement. But with a fresh perspective and a good dose of out-of-the-box thinking, Sörbo proved it could be better. It was different, even strange, but it made a window cleaner's job easier and more profitable. A new line of products was spawned that no one else imagined could exist... products that changed the way window cleaning was done.

When everyone else simply accepted that cleaning French windows was always going to be a painful, time-consuming process, Sörbo created the Multi-Squeegee®. His unusual, but highly effective creation, cut the labor in half. He did the same for cleaning louvered windows with the Tricket®. With the Eliminator®, large expanses of storefront glass could be cleaned with one simple stroke. These are just a few ideas that sprang out of his desire to make window cleaning easier from the bottom up... from the perspective of real window cleaners.

Sörbo Samuelsson is the last of the initial window cleaner breed and is becoming one of its biggest names due to inventing and manufacturing the most Innovative Window Cleaning Equipment in the industry.

Made in the USA
Monee, IL
27 March 2025

14240693R00174